His Days With BAPU

Gandhiji's Personal Secretary

Shobha Warrier

Vitastaa

Let Knowledge Spread

Published by
Renu Kaul Verma
Vitasta Publishing Pvt Ltd
2/15, Ansari Road, Daryaganj
New Delhi - 110 002
info@vitastapublishing.com

ISBN 978-93-82711-87-2

First Edition 2015
Second Reprint 2024
MRP ₹350

The views and opinions expressed in this book are the protagonist's own. The author is solely responsible for the facts and authenticity of the quotes and sources used for this work. The publisher is in no way liable for the same.

Typeset by Vits Press
Printed by Vikas Computer and Printers

Contents

To my Dearest Soman

Letters from all over the world used to reach wherever Bapu was. Even if the address had just Mahatma Gandhi, India, it reached Sevagram

Acknowledgements

I have to first thank Kalyanamji for setting his daily routine aside and spending hours upon hours talking to me in spite of his age. He was extremely patient with me.

Many thanks are due to my publisher Renu Kaul Verma for supporting this idea. Thank you, Papri, for being my friend and my editor. If Saraswathi hadn't spent an enormous amount of effort transcribing my conversations with Kalyanamji, I would not have been able to write this book anywhere near as quickly as I have been able to. Thank you, Saraswathi!

Thank you, Sreeram Selvaraj, for spending many hours taking pictures of the old photos from Kalyanam's collection, for the book.

And finally, thanks go out to my dear son, Siddhu. Now that my husband Soman is no longer with us, Siddhu took his place and spent hours as the first reader and editor of this book.

The author and publisher also acknowledge reference material taken from Creative Commons resources like Wikipedia and Google, and contributions of artistes whose work is available on the net. Photographs used here are taken from V Kalyanam's collection of photographs, more than 60 years ago.

Most of Mahatma Gandhi's quotes are taken from http://www.gandhiashramsevagram.org/

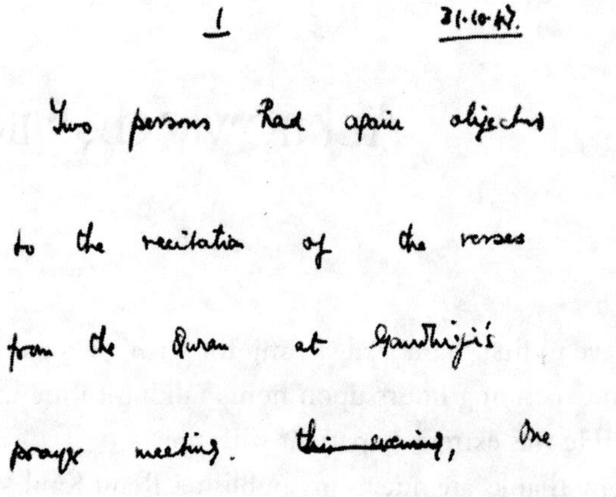

1 31-10-47.

Two persons had again objected to the recitation of the verses from the Quran at Gandhiji's prayer meeting. ~~this evening~~, One of the objectors being the same who had objected the previous evening. Both were gently restrained in their objection. G. asked the audience if it was not proper on his part to hold the prayer ~~because that~~ one or two men out of several thousands objected

Kalyanam was supposed to write what transpired at the prayer meetings to be sent to the newspapers. In this article dated 31-10-47, Kalyanam writes that two persons objected to the reciting of the verses from the Koran

Foreword

It is a door that never closes. While the 93-year-old Kalyanam tells all of his puzzled visitors that there is nothing expensive behind the open door, the house is full of invaluable treasures, 'treasures today's India has never seen or heard of.' This is how the author's note in this gem of a book begins. And from the very first page one is engrossed in, and enriched by the treasures that it unfolds page after page.

This book, written by Shobha Warrier, is a riveting biographical sketch of a unique man who lived under fifteen prime ministers—some of whom he knew personally. Despite his frail health, this personal secretary of Bapu from 1944-1948, set his daily routine of gardening and cleanliness aside, and spent hours talking to the author, and this is how the book happened.

Divided into three parts, the book relates the story of this extraordinary personal secretary of Bapu, who stepped into the shoes of Mahadev Desai [his personal secretary for twenty five years and whose death in 1942 had been a colossal loss to Bapu].

In the first section , we are told of Kalyanam's life before Bapu, his small role in the Quit India Movement, going to Sevagram in 1943, meeting Bapu in 1944 and later becoming his personal secretary and being privy to his everyday life for four years [1944- 1948], until his assassination. The last section tells us about his days after Bapu, when he worked with many famous people, including Pt Jawaharlal Nehru, Rajagopalachari, Lady Mountbatten and Mirabehn. This small book encapsulates a wealth of details about Bapu, who he 'had the divine opportunity to work and live under', having been initiated into his first lessons in non-violence when he stepped into Sevagram Ashram in 1943.

Aghast on seeing a centipede crawling on the floor, he crushed it to pulp, and was told in no uncertain terms that this belligerence would not be tolerated as, 'This is Bapu's ashram, nobody kills an insect here.' As Bapu's personal secretary, he was with him from the crack of dawn to night, endlessly taking notes, writing letters, being at the receiving end of many an affectionate reprimand, and also being by his side when those bullets which ended the life of so great a man, were fired.

The last section, written in first person, carries Kalayanam's views on—Bapu and today's India, corruption, Swachch Bharat, Patel and Nehru and the different prime ministers of India .

A dejected Bapu, towards the end of his life had remarked, 'My voice is in the wilderness. My writ runs no more. The government does not listen to me. I am not the current coin that I fancied I once was.'

Reading this book, I found myself hoping with Kalyanam that the world should be deluged with what Bapu stood for, that his voice, with that feathery softness, should no longer remain a voice in the wilderness, and he should continue to be a much-valued coin in the present insanely materialistic world.

Written with a sincere effortlessness, Kalyanam's transparent honesty shines through Shobha Warrier's labour of love. Making no efforts at holding a plea for Bapu's idiosyncrasies, his fads and foibles, Kalyanam remarks that one had no option but to learn to live with him and his whimsicalities.

One never tires of reading more and more about the extraordinary man that Bapu was. This book not only tells us some interesting and lesser known facts about Bapu, but also about another man, whom Rajagopachari called, 'remarkable', and who served Bapu selflessly for four years, being privy to his anguish of the last days, when he no longer wanted to live for one hundred and twenty five years, as his beloved country had started following the doctrine of the sword, which he had abhorred all his life.

Warrier has indeed done a commendable job by enlightening the world about this self-effacing secretary of Bapu, who, even at the ripe old age of ninety-three, is obsessed with gardening and cleanliness, and believes, like Bapu, that India can become really Swachch, only if everyone becomes his own scavenger.

She says: 'Very few get the opportunity like Kalyanam did to walk amongst giants as they shaped the destinies of a subcontinent. As time passes, there are fewer and fewer like him left walking the face of the planet—men and women who bore close witness to some of Indian history's most tumultuous years.'

Hence, this book, embellished with some interesting snippets about those tumultuous years, some intriguing facts, some brutal home truths, will indeed be an invaluable treasure for every college and university library and is highly recommend for both, the young and old.

—Dr Santosh Bakaya

Poet, essayist , novelist and writer of *Ballad of Bapu*

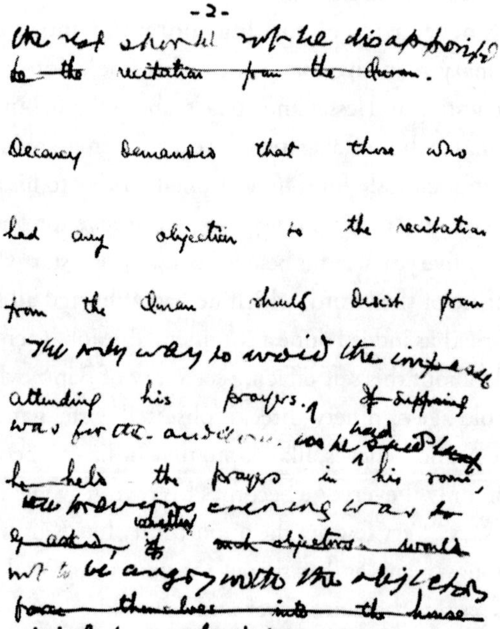

-2-

the rest should not be disapproving

~~to the recitation from the Quran.~~

Decency demanded that those who had any objection to the recitation from the Quran should desist from

The only way to avoid the impasse

attending his prayers. ~~If suffering~~

was for the audience. He had ~~agreed~~

~~he held the prayers in his room,~~

~~the following~~ evening was to

~~be asked, if~~ whether ~~such objectors would~~

not to be angry with the objectors

~~force themselves into the house~~

& not to molest them in any

way whatsoever. He also

~~and dissuade him from praying.~~

asked the police not to interfere

In the second page of the article, Kalyanam writes that Gandhiji told those who had objection to the recitation that they should desist from attending his prayer meetings

Author's Note

V. Kalyanam, Mahatma Gandhi's Personal Secretary': the name board on the door smiles at you.

It's a door that never closes. While 93-year-old Kalyanam tells all of his puzzled visitors that there is nothing expensive behind the open door, the house is full of invaluable treasures; treasures today's India has never seen or heard of.

In the house are trunks full of cuttings from the pre-independence era and the explosive first days of freedom that followed. The trunk holds photos of Bapu with many leaders of the era. Most importantly, though, they hold copies of letters — letters written in the Mahatma's own hand and typed up letters he has corrected.

When I first met Kalyanam in the late 1990s, he had hundreds of letters written in Bapu's hand which he was planning to give to a foreigner, after all the museums he had contacted refused to accept them. He felt as he grew older, it was not possible for him to keep them safe at home. His decision created a furore in the country but it served the purpose; the Nehru Museum at Teen Murti Bhavan accepted them and now they are on display there.

Kalyanam describes himself as a person who 'had the divine

opportunity to work and learn under Gandhiji', having started off as a stenographer and soon growing to become his personal secretary, from 1944 until his assassination in January 1948.

As there is hardly anyone alive in India today who had had this 'divine' opportunity, it is also a divine opportunity for a journalist like me to meet such a man and listen to the stories he has to tell.

At the time I first met him, Kalyanamji was more agile and sprightly than he is today, with his slight stoop and the need to walk hesitantly with the aid of a stick. But physical infirmity has not dampened his obsession with cleanliness. His day starts at 3 in the morning with a cup of coffee that he brews for himself. Then starts his mission in life; that to clean. No wonder he calls himself a 'sweeper par excellence', a term he coined well before the rest of India started talking about cleanliness and Swachch Bharat [Clean India].

From early morning, he spends all his time cleaning the house, the common areas of his apartment building, and the road, before going on to tend to the plants in his garden and terrace. With age catching up, he gave up on sweeping the road at the age of ninety-three .

But he is an angry old man these days; angry because he feels Indians have no respect for cleanliness and discipline. That is why he decided to write to the Prime Minister appreciating his efforts to make India a 'Swachch Bharat'. But he also warned Narendra Modi that success in the mission might well be difficult to achieve.

In the six months I took to write the book, I saw his health deteriorate gradually. A fall on the terrace that resulted in a broken arm made him all the more weaker, and he began to forget names, incidents and dates. He says, 'Ageing and absentmindedness go hand in hand. I am afflicted with absentmindedness. Maybe in due course, I may even forget that I ever worked with Gandhiji.'

As I prodded him for more details on his extraordinary life, he told me several times, 'You came to me ten years late... I am the only person from the old Gandhi camp who is still alive, and I amninety-three!'

Yes, I also wish the idea of this book occurred to me a few years ago...

He was an employee of the British Indian Government in New Delhi when he accidentally got involved in the Quit India movement. This led to the man who'd never liked secretarial work heading to Sevagram to undertake the menial labour he preferred in Gandhiji's own ashram. But destiny and Gandhi had other plans. Bapu made Kalyanam his personal secretary with the responsibility of writing all of his correspondence!

Though this book is about Kalyanam's days with Bapu, I have decided to start the story at a point before he, a callow youth at the time, barely knew of the Mahatma. That is when the extraordinary journey began, on the streets of New Delhi in the August of 1942. An extraordinary journey it was, as the young man who was more British than the British transformed himself into a close associate of Mahatma Gandhi, wore khadi and worked closely with all the leaders who fought against the British for India's independence.

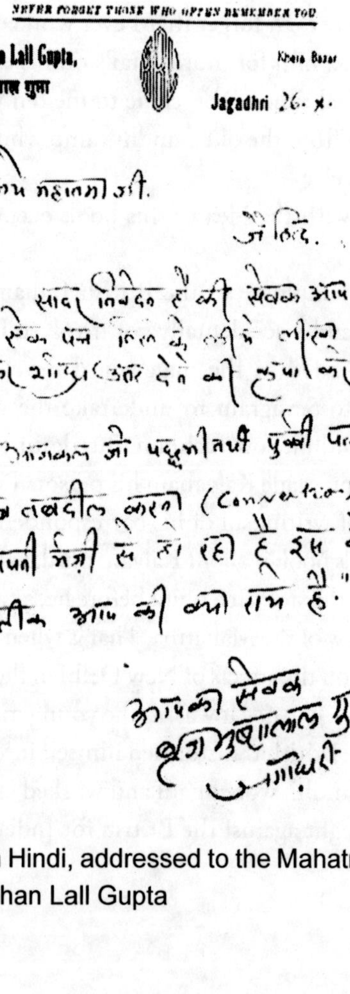

NEVER FORGET THOSE WHO OFTEN REMEMBER YOU

Brij Bhushan Lall Gupta,
बृजभूषणलाल गुप्ता

Khera Bazar

Jagadhri 26. x. 1947.

श्री पूज्य महात्मा जी.

जै हिन्द.

सादर निवेदन है की सेवक आप की सेवा में यह सवाल पेश करता है जिस को ले के लाचार रहा है. कृपा कर आदेश/उत्तर देने की कृपा करें.

"आजकल जो पाकिस्तानी पूर्वी पंजाब में मज़हब तबदील करना (Conversion) ज़बरदस्ती या अपनी मर्ज़ी से हो रहा है इस के मुतल्लिक आप की क्या राय है."

आपका सेवक
बृजभूषणलाल गुप्ता
जगाधरी

A letter in Hindi, addressed to the Mahatma from Brij Bhushan Lall Gupta

His Days before Bapu

Ninety-three years ago, on the 15th of August, a son was born to Venkatram and Meenambal, a Tamil couple living in Delhi and Shimla. It was not unusual for people from the south of India to move to Delhi for work in those days. They were very good at typing and stenography, and the British were appreciative of their work ethic and knowledge of English.

It was in 1914, when the First World War was raging, that the young Venkatram moved to Delhi to work for the British. Very soon, he married Meenambal, who too began to live with him in Delhi. In 1922, their first son was born; a boy they named Kalyanam.

In those days, Shimla was the summer capital of the British. The entire apparatus of British rule in India, from the Viceroy down to the lowest peon, upped stakes and moved from Delhi to Shimla each summer.

It was during the course of one such summer in India that Venkatram decided to start a similarly peripatetic school for the children of the South Indians whose parents worked for the Raj. It was then called the Madrasi School.

When Kalyanam started going to that school, the primary school had just twelve students. Today, the school is called the Delhi Tamil Educational Association High School. From 1971, the school is called DTEA Senior Secondary School. As the school also moved with the people from Delhi to Shimla, and back with the change of season, Kalyanam too spent his school days shuttling between Delhi and Shimla.

Kalyanam then went on to study Commerce in a college in Delhi before following his father's footsteps to get a job with the British government.

Surprisingly, the nationalist movement that reverberated across the country did not have any impact on the young Kalyanam as a student. It was only after he joined the service of the British that he started to read the newspapers. Once he picked up the habit of newspaper reading, he found that all of them were full of stories about a man called Mohandas Karamchand Gandhi who wanted independence for the country. This made him wonder why this Gandhi wished to drive the British away.

'I cared not a whit about who ruled India. At one time, we were under the Mughals, who were followed by the British. Under the British, I felt we had a good government. Even Gandhi admitted it. He had said, "Good government is no substitute for self-government." This implied that he wanted self-government for its sake, and not because he felt the current government was bad.'

So anglicised and so much in awe of the British was young Kalyanam that he never stepped out without a tie and hat. Though he lived like a Briton, with affected mannerisms that were more British than the British, his family was in touch with the other southern immigrants in Delhi.

'In those days, there were nearly three thousand South Indians in Delhi. But yet, all of us knew each other and helped each other out. The majority of the people who worked in the Secretariat were South Indians, pejoratively called Madrasis, irrespective of whether they came from Kerala, Karnataka or Andhra Pradesh. The joke going around Delhi in those days was that the government consisted purely of Madrasis and chaprasis (peons).'

Kalyanam remembers that the camaraderie among the people of south India was so strong that if there were a wedding or any such function in any South Indian family, the rest of the families would take time off work to help them. 'Somebody would be in charge of the kitchen, another would chop the vegetables up, some others would do the cooking, and yet some others would serve coffee and food to the guests. Not a single servant or cook would be employed. All of the work was done by the community.'

He was just twenty-two then, and the Quit India Movement had started. That was when he did something he never imagined he would do. It was a tiny favour for a group of his South Indian friends who worked for the British Raj, yet wanted to be a small part of Mahatma Gandhi's nationalist movement.

The Quit India Movement 1942

The Second World War started on 1 September 1939 with Hitler's panzers rolling into Poland, leading France and Britain to declare war on Germany. In the September 1939 meeting of the Congress Working Committee in Wardha, Maharashtra, the Congress Party passed a resolution offering their conditional support to the British Empire's fight against fascism, subject to India receiving independence at the end of the war. But the British government refused to entertain this.The Indian nationalist movement's refusal to cooperate with the British war effort led the British government to send the Cripps Mission in March 1942 (led by the left-wing Labour leader, Sir Stafford Cripps) to India to negotiate with the Indian National Congress for full cooperation in the War in return for full self-government after the war. However, the talks failed. Upon the failure of the talks, Mahatma Gandhi said, 'The British intend to continue their old policy of divide and rule. The Congress has asked for bread and it has received a stone in return.' In May 1942, Gandhi asked Britain to 'leave India to God. If this is too much to ask, then leave her to anarchy.' On 14 July 1942, the Congress Working Committee passed the resolution that demanded 'the immediate ending of the British

> rule in India'. Gandhi's mantra was to 'do or die'... Mahatma Gandhi asked his colleagues to come up with the right slogan for the mass civil disobedience movement planned. When one of them suggested 'Get Out', Gandhi rejected it as impolite. Rajagopalachari suggested 'Retreat' or 'Withdraw' which also did not get Gandhiji's approval. When Yusuf Meheraly presented Gandhi a bow with an inscription bearing the words 'Quit India', he liked it. That was how the historic slogan known to every Indian schoolchild was selected. Thus it came to be that on the 8th of August 1942, Mahatma Gandhi launched the Quit India movement asking the British to leave India. He added, 'At a time when I may have to launch the biggest struggle of my life, I do not harbour hatred against anybody.' In the early hours of the 9th of August, all of the top leadership of the Congress, including leading lights such as Gandhi, Jawaharlal Nehru, Sardar Vallabhbhai Patel and Maulana Azad were arrested. And the Congress was declared an unlawful organisation by the British government.

Kalyanam readily agreed to distribute the nationalist pamphlets when some of his South Indian friends asked him to. His task was to slip the pamphlets under the doors of every house that did not belong to an Englishman. After 10 o'clock at night, unobserved by the police, Kalyanam quietly slipped out to distribute the pamphlets. 'There were about a hundred houses in my area. So I was given around fifty pamphlets to distribute to start with. On the first night, I must have delivered around twenty. After that I came home satisfied and slept.'

He performed the same task on the second night too. But on the third night, his luck ran out. As he was delivering a pamphlet under a door, he was caught hold of by a police sergeant. 'In those days, police sergeants were all Anglo-Indians; most of them hefty fellows. When he saw me distributing the pamphlets, he stopped his motorbike, walked towards me and asked, "What is it you're doing?" I said, "I am slipping a paper under this house's door." The angry Sergeant retorted, "Do you know what's in the paper?" I admitted to not having read it myself. He picked up the paper, read it and said, "You are committing treason; you are asking the British to quit India." I didn't know what to say.'

The Police Sergeant arrested Kalyanam for participating in treasonous activities and he was taken to the Connaught Place police station in Delhi where he saw many arrested Congressmen sitting, all huddled together. The Police kept Kalyanam there for the night. When Kalyanam informed his father that he had been arrested and detained by the police, his father just kept quiet as though he had been expecting it.

The next day, on the 14th of August 1942, he was transferred to Lahore jail along with the other arrested Congressmen. Kalyanam ended up spending nine whole months in jail. 'I didn't attach any importance to the arrest itself. Arrests were very common in those days. I went to jail without an iota of fear in my mind. I was also treated very well. Unlike some of the others arrested, I was not involved in violence like cutting off electric wires or removing railway tracks. In comparison, I was harmless. I had only distributed pamphlets, which was a very minor offence. While many of the others were beaten up, the jail authorities did not take much notice of me. I enjoyed my time there, playing ping-pong and volleyball in the evenings. They also gave me good food. After nine months, when they found that I was a well-behaved boy, they let me go.'

So Kalyanam returned to Delhi from Lahore to be with his family. But he'd lost his government job at the Secretariat, in spite of the fact that his English boss was very sympathetic to the Indian nationalist cause. However, Kalyanam had become an employee who had turned against the establishment that gave him his salary.... So, Kalyanam found another job with an insurance company for a salary of sixty rupees in no time.

The turning point in Kalyanam's life occurred during this period. It was his introduction to a man named Devdas Gandhi, who happened to be Mahatma Gandhi's fourth son and C Rajagopalachari's son-in-law.

Devdas Gandhi was then the Managing Editor of the Hindustan Times newspaper. A friend of Kalyanam's father told Devdas Gandhi about a young man who hated secretarial work but was forced to do just that. What impressed Devdas Gandhi was that the young man wanted to do menial labour and spent his evenings working for the poor.

'I always wanted to clean and sweep. It was my hobby. I learnt to do cleaning work from my British neighbour who used to work in the garden, paint his house and work in the kitchen after coming back home from work. I enjoyed doing such work. To this day, I derive great pleasure from the act of cleaning. I am fanatical about keeping the premises I live in, very clean, devoid of any dirt. When my father's friend told Devdas Gandhi about me, the latter expressed a desire to meet me. That was how my life changed.'

The first question Devdas Gandhi asked Kalyanam when they met was, 'Why don't you go to Sevagram Ashram? The ashram is the place where you can do menial labour. I am sure you will enjoy the ambience.' The funny thing was that Kalyanam did not know then that Sevagram Ashram belonged to Mahatma Gandhi and Devdas Gandhi was Mahatma Gandhi's son. 'Nobody told me who Devdas Gandhi was and he did not tell me who lived in the ashram. I thought he was sending me to some ashram.'

It was just before the trip that another turning point in his life happened. His British boss's wife requested him to accompany her to the Khadi Bhandar in Chandni Chowk as an interpreter. An admirer of khadi material, she wanted to buy the material to make a dress for herself. While she chose the material, Kalyanam went around and bought a handkerchief and a towel for three rupees and a khadi kurta and pyjama for nineteen rupees. From that day onwards, he decided to bid adieu to suits and ties and started wearing kurta-pyjamas instead.

Kalyanam was delighted when his new British boss, who was also 'quite sympathetic to Mahatma Gandhi's call for swaraj', granted him leave for two months to go and live in Sevagram Ashram. 'When my boss warned me that there would be no servants at the ashram and I would have to do all the sweeping, cleaning, and gardening by myself, the idea of joining an ashram grew even more fascinating.' So he was all set to start a new life in Sevagram Ashram; a life that would bring him face-to-face with Mahatma Gandhi.

Occasions like the present do not occur in everybody's and but rarely in anybody's life. I want you to know and feel that there is nothing but purest Ahimsa in all that I am saying and doing today. The draft resolution of the Working Committee is based on Ahimsa, the contemplated struggle similarly has its roots in Ahimsa. If, therefore, there is any among you who has lost faith in Ahimsa or is wearied of it, let him not vote for this resolution. Let me explain my position clearly. God has vouchsafed to me a priceless gift in the weapon of Ahimsa. I and my Ahimsa are on our trial today. If in the present crisis, when the earth is being scorched by the flames of 'himsa' and crying for deliverance, I failed to make use of the God-given talent, God will not forgive me and I shall be judged unworthy of the great gift. I must act now.

—Mahatma Gandhi

Mahatma Gandhi and Kasturba in Sevagram before Kalyanam went there

Off to Sevagram

Until the year 1930, the Sabarmati Ashram in Gujarat was what Mahatma Gandhi called home. On an early morning of the 12th of March that year, he and seventy-nine other inmates of the ashram, began the march to Dandi, Gujarat, to break the discriminatory law that maintained a British monopoly on the production of salt in India and raised up to 8.2% of the British Raj's revenue. After making salt in contravention of the British law in Dandi, Gandhiji continued his march southwards, whereupon he was arrested and taken to Yerwada jail on the 4th of May 1930. He was held there until the 26th of January 1931. Upon his release, he took a vow never to return to the Sabarmati Ashram until India had gained her independence. But he never returned to Sabarmati at all. In 1934, when Gandhiji expressed his desire to live amongst villagers and help them with their lives, Jamnalal Bajaj, an industrialist, philanthropist and freedom fighter, invited him to his house in Wardha, Maharashtra. Bajaj offered him the option to stay at Segaon, a small village around 8 km from Wardha, that belonged to him. Gandhiji decided to walk to the village on the 30th of April 1936. Mahadev Desai (Gandhiji's personal secretary), Jamnalal Bajaj, Shriman Narayan and Balwant Sinha joined him on the walk. As no houses were ready for him to take residence, Gandhiji rested inside an improvised bamboo hut in the midst of some guava trees. Jamnalal Bajaj ensured the construction of a hut for Gandhiji in no time. The great man himself occupied one corner of it, while the second was given over to his wife Kasturba. The third corner was reserved for Mahadev Desai, while the fourth was kept aside for guests who came to meet Gandhiji. For several months, Khan Abdul Ghaffar Khan, the Pashtun Indian nationalist variously known as the Frontier Gandhi and Badshah Khan, stayed in this fourth corner. This hut is today known as Adi Niwas. As the village did not have a post or telegraph office in those days, hundreds of letters addressed to Gandhi were brought from Wardha to the village. But since letters to Segaon were often misdirected to the similarly named Shegaon, the decision was taken in 1940 to rename Segaon to Sevagram (the village of service). Gandhiji lived in Sevagram until 1946 and never returned to Sevagram after that.

In October 1943, Kalyanam, dressed in kurta pyjama with just one suitcase in tow, began his journey from Delhi to Wardha, in the third class compartment of the Grand Trunk Express. Though he had two thousand rupees (a large amount in those days) saved in his bank account, he took just a hundred rupees with him. As he was assured of boarding and lodging at the ashram, he knew he wouldn't need to carry much money on his person. Soon, he found that a Sevagram inmate didn't need to spend even a single paisa at the ashram. But that's a story for later…

After a two-day journey, the train reached Wardha Junction, where Devdas Gandhi had told him to alight. Kalyanam looked around and found to his dismay that there was no one to receive him at the station. He caught hold of a tonga (horse carriage) and continued the rest of the journey in it. 'The road was so bumpy and dusty that I still get nightmares thinking about the 8-km journey that took me a whole hour! By the time, I got there, I was covered in mud and dust', Kalyanam recalls.

Finally, he was standing in front of the ashram he'd dreamt of for weeks; it was a vast expanse of land with many huts spread out. He went to the office and presented the introduction letter from Devdas Gandhi to the Sevagram manager. He had written in the letter that Kalyanam was well versed in English and Hindi, and would like to do all kinds of work there.

'The Manager started talking to me in Hindi but soon switched over to English. I was a bit shocked when he told one of the men, "Show him to his hut." The man then took me to a hut! That was the first time in my life that I was seeing a hut. I had always lived in a good house with indoor plumbing; a luxury in those days.'

The hut assigned to Kalyanam was a thatched one with a door that could not be locked. Later, he came to know that in the ashram, everything was simple and open as no one expected to find a thief there.

'The man who came with me opened the door and I saw to my surprise that the walls were made of bricks that were covered with packed mud. The floor was pasted with cow dung! But everything looked so clean and neat. I was asked to leave my slippers outside before entering the room. We had taken just two steps in when I saw a centipede moving on the floor. My immediate reaction was to step back, take my slippers and hit it with my slippers. I hit it so hard that it turned into chutney. The man who accompanied me was horrified to see what I had done. Shocked, he asked me, "What have you done?"'

'I said, "It is a dangerous insect! I had to kill it." He said, "You will find not just centipedes but even scorpions and snakes here. But this is Bapu's Ashram; nobody kills even an insect here. Everybody has to observe non-violence."'

That was Kalyanam's first lesson in non-violence. The person then told him that Bapu and the other leaders were in jail, which was why there were only half a dozen people at the ashram.

After travelling for two days in the train with very little food, Kalyanam was very hungry but he didn't know who to ask for food. 'I had only seen women in the kitchen at my house. But I could not find a single woman anywhere in the ashram. I wondered who would be doing the cooking and whether I would get any food. I was very hungry. Reading my face, the man who accompanied me told me that there was a common kitchen where every inmate would have to go for food when the bell rang.'

So no food until then!

What Kalyanam needed more urgently was a visit to the toilet and a bath but he noticed that none of the huts had electricity, water supply or toilets. 'I felt hunger could wait. So I asked him where the toilet was. He took me to a row of dozen or so small huts outside and said they were the toilets. They were about four feet across, partitioned, and with thatched doors. Again, none of the doors was bolted. The man told me I could just close the door and use it without fear of anyone barging in. I had to trust him on that!'

What he saw inside the toilet booth was a 5-foot-deep pit called a trench latrine. Naturally, the city-bred Kalyanam was initially shocked to see such a toilet. In Delhi, he had only used commodes.'There were two stones for you to squat on and defecate. Close to them was a heap of mud, a coconut shell and a spade made of bamboo. After you finished the job, you were to take two or three heaps of mud using the coconut shell, and cover your poop with it. But what surprised me was that the toilets did not stink, and there wasn't a single fly or mosquito to be seen. There was a bowl of water in a corner to wash up after the deed. This was the most ingenious toilet I had ever seen in my life.

Even today, I feel that this is an example that people in Indian villages where people defecate in the open can emulate.' He soon learnt that when the pit got filled to the point that it was just a foot deep, people stopped using it and covered it completely with mud. In about six-seven months, the contents of the pit would have turned into compost that the ashram used as fertiliser. Once the compost was taken out, the pit was used as a toilet once again.

Then, it was time for a bath. He had to bathe out in the open, next to a well that everybody was expected to draw water out of.

As he finished his bath, the kitchen bell rang. It was music to the ears of the hungry Kalyanam. At this point, everybody in the ashram silently ran into the kitchen, grabbed a plate, washed it, and then collected the food.

The food was simple—just chapatis, rice, dal and some vegetables. After eating, each inmate washed his own plate, as well as one of the vessels used to cook the food, to help the kitchen volunteers out. That night, he was told that no coffee or tea was served in the morning. But inmates were permitted to make tea in their own huts; an option some took up. What everyone did get in the morning was hot water, lime and two tablespoons of honey; a drink the Mahatma himself preferred.

Plenty of fruits like oranges, bananas and papayas were grown at the ashram. The inmates were encouraged to eat them. 'There were many orange trees in the ashram and we could pluck oranges from the tree ourselves. We used to eat papayas in the mornings as they were supposed to be very good for your health', Kalyanam remembers. At Sevagram, the inmates did not have to spend a single paisa on clothing as they were encouraged to spin their own clothes.

Kalyanam soon realised that there were only a few people like him at the ashram who spoke English; most of the others were uneducated. 'Many of the poor folk from the nearby villages had joined the ashram for free food. For example, the cooks were mostly illiterate villagers who were quite happy to cook for everyone.'

'Everybody could choose his or her own role at the ashram, depending on each one's interests and abilities. If someone was a good cook, he was put in charge of the kitchen. If he was good at milking cows, he would be in charge of the cattle. There were people involved in making soap, paper and many other handcrafted products. Those who wanted to teach were assigned the task of teaching at a basic school in the village. There was also a dispensary for the villages nearby where inmates worked.'

As Kalyanam had gone there to undertake menial labour, he began to work in the garden and fields without anyone telling him to. 'I didn't care about what was going on in the ashram; I just worked. I used to go to the vegetable garden and fields in the morning after having my lemon water and work there for three-four hours. When the sun rose high in the sky, I would come back, have my bath and eat a papaya plucked from the garden.'

Even today, Kalyanam feels that the self-sufficient ashram was a kind of model village. 'There was no furniture in any of the huts; no beverages were served except papaya juice and milk. Everything about the ashram was transparent. Yes, they followed a set of rules as one does in a hostel but everything was for the common good. Everyone practised economy and simple living. Nobody was allowed to waste anything, especially food. They followed what Gandhiji said, "Eat to live; do not live to eat." Above all, there was dignity of labour. In short, ashram life was for those who wanted to lead a simple, free, contented, healthy life, with no desire to amass wealth. I felt at home and enjoyed the long hours spent toiling.'

After a few days, the ashram Manager asked him to do some work in the office as he knew English well. At least thirty to forty letters addressed to Gandhiji reached the ashram every day, as he was not permitted to receive correspondence in jail. 'There were letters from all over India, from every province, asking something or the other of Gandhi. Letters arrived from Germany, Italy, France, South Africa—all over the world, in fact. Some of them were simply addressed to "Mr. Gandhi, India". Even if the address said, "Mr Gandhi, Calcutta", the letters were routed through to the Sevagram Ashram. My job was to segregate the letters language-wise and tie them up into little bundles. I never read any of the letters, as they were all addressed to Gandhiji.' But Kalyanam had to learn from the Manager how to open the letters. The first time, when he tore open a letter, the angry Manager told him that he had just wasted the envelope. But he didn't understand how he'd done that!

'The Manager then showed me how to cut it open carefully so that the unused side could be used by Gandhiji for writing. That was done on Gandhiji's instructions as he didn't like to waste anything.'

Everyone in the ashram called Gandhiji, Bapu. Kalyanam too began to use the term to refer to the Mahatma. As each day passed, his desire to meet the man himself grew. For that, however, he had to wait a while longer.

He alone deserves to be called an inmate of the Ashram who has ceased to have any worldly relation—a relation involving monetary interests—with his parents or other relatives, who has no other needs save those of food and clothing and who is ever watchful in the observance of the eleven cardinal vows. Therefore, he who needs to make savings should never be regarded as an Ashram inmate.

—Mahatma Gandhi

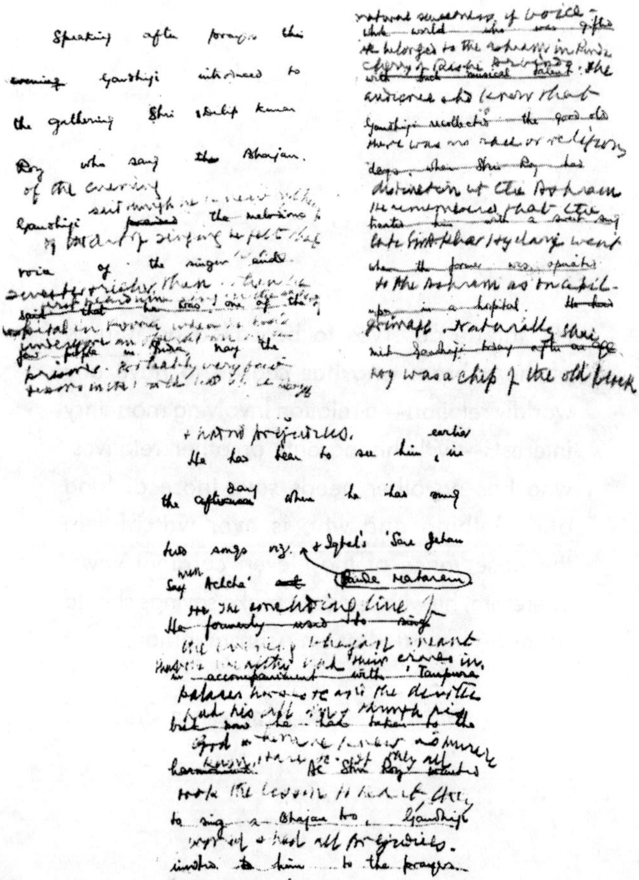
Speaking after prayer this evening Gandhiji introduced to the gathering Shri Dilip Kumar Roy who sang the Bhajan of the evening.

Roy was a chip of the old block

He has been to see him earlier in the afternoon when he has sung two songs viz. Iqbal's 'Sare Jahan Se Achcha' and 'Vande Mataram'

to sing a Bhajan too. Gandhiji

invited him to the prayers.

Notes written by Kalyanam on the prayer meeting in which he speaks about introducing Dilip Kumar Roy, who sang bhajans and the songs *Saare jahan se achcha* and *Vande Mataram*. Gandhiji made corrections in them.

Meeting the Mahatma
1944

Following their arrests in August 1942 after the launch of the Quit India movement, Mahatma Gandhi, his wife Kasturba, his personal secretaries Mahadev Desai and Pyarelal Nayyar, his personal physician Sushila Nayyar, his British disciple Mirabehn (born Madeleine Slade, daughter of the British Rear-Admiral, Sir Edmond Slade), and the poet and freedom fighter Sarojini Naidu were interned at the Aga Khan Palace in Pune.The 50-year old Mahadev Desai, who had served Gandhiji as his personal secretary and advisor for twenty-five years, succumbed to a heart attack a mere six days after his arrest. A devastated Gandhiji lit Desai's funeral pyre himself. After suffering

> two heart attacks in January, his wife Kasturba too passed away while still imprisoned on 22 February 1944. Following these personal losses, Gandhiji also fell ill.

When Kalyanam made his way to the Sevagram Ashram in October 1943, Gandhiji was interned at the Aga Khan Palace in Pune. However, when he fell ill in jail in May 1944, he was released unconditionally by the British, and he decided to go to Bombay for treatment.

'The news of his illness spread gloom in the ashram. This happened three months after Kasturba had died of malaria. Penicillin had been discovered in England in 1928, but it wasn't widely available in India. When Kasturba fell ill, Devdas Gandhi imported penicillin from London and took it to the Aga Khan Palace, but Gandhiji refused to give it to her. He was totally against allopathic treatment. He said, "If God wants her to live, she will live." Everybody felt that she would have survived if she had been given the medicine. Anyway, she passed away in February. In May 1944, three months after Kasturba's death, Bapu fell ill. Her death affected him badly; after all, they were together from a very young age [they were married when they were both just thirteen].'

When he too fell ill, Gandhi refused to take any of the allopathic medicines on offer on account of his belief in natural remedies. Naturally, the British establishment panicked. Worried that his death in jail could result in a frenzy of riots erupting all across India, they decided to quietly release him on the 5th of May, to undertake whatever course of treatment he wished to take.

Kalyanam still admires the British for taking good care of the Mahatma. 'When he was alive, the British took every step to see that he was well cared for. They considered him a very great man, despite the fact that he fought against British rule. In fact, he was a friend of the British. He was only against British rule, and not the British people. There were many English ladies working with us in the ashram, the most well-known of whom was Mirabehn [Madeleine Slade].'

The ill Bapu went to Bombay first where he stayed with Shanti Kumar Morarjee, a shipping magnate known for his philanthropic activities, in his big bungalow in Juhu.

The moment Bapu landed at Morarjee's house in Bombay, there was excitement in the ashram as it had been nearly two years since any of the ashramites had met him. When some of the people who managed the ashram decided to go to Bombay to see him, Kalyanam also expressed his desire to tag along, for he had not yet seen the great man in person. The band of travellers agreed to take him with them.

'We all went by train to Bombay and from the station, we went straight to a hotel. After a shower and some food, we took a bus to where Bapu was staying. I was expecting a huge crowd outside, but there was nobody near the gate. I was told that his stay there was being kept a secret for the moment. We opened the gate and quietly made our way in. On the ground floor, inside a room, I saw a very old man in a loincloth standing and talking to a well-dressed man. I did not realise the old man was Gandhiji.'

Kalyanam thought the man who was dressed like an Englishman was the master of the house and the old man in the loincloth was his servant! 'Imagine! I mistook the Mahatma for a servant. I thought the boss was giving instructions to the servant to do something. I expected a great man like him to be dressed in a suit, with a necktie. It was stupid of me to think so but then I was young and inexperienced. Moreover, I had seen the letters he'd written in English at the ashram and could not square a man as well-versed in English as all that with this old man in a loincloth.'

Bapu recognised all of the inmates of the ashram except Kalyanam, who stood quietly outside the room waiting for him to finish the conversation. Once the conversation ended, Bapu slowly walked in and sat on a mattress kept in a corner of the room. Next to the mattress was a small desk with some papers, a pen and a bottle of water on it.

Kalyanam remembers his first encounter with Bapu quite clearly even today. 'He was in his loincloth and looked extremely weak; so much so I saw his hand tremble as he lifted a pen. He sat down on the mattress and asked all of us to come in. Even then, I hadn't figured out who he was. Like a fool, I just wondered why the people in my group were standing so respectfully in front of him.'

Then his fellow ashramites introduced Kalyanam to Gandhiji as a 'young Madrasi boy from Delhi sent by Devdas Gandhi' to join the ashram. 'They said, "His name is Kalyanam, Madrasi ladka hain." They added that I liked working in the ashram. I just stood there looking at him. He looked at me and started talking to me. He didn't have his dentures on, so I heard only a sibilant shushing sound—shsh shsh shsh. He talked in such a low voice that I had to bend down to catch his words. Even then, I could not comprehend what he wanted to know.'

Somehow, Kalyanam managed to decipher the first question to him, 'Tumhara Naam Kya Hain?' He told the Mahatma his name. Then Bapu asked, 'Ashram mein kaam karte ho? Do you like it?' Kalyanam replied that he did. Gandhiji's next question was, 'Tumhare ma baap kya karte hain?' Each time he asked something, Kalyanam bent down to hear him clearly. When he did so the third time, Gandhiji waved to him to sit down next to him.

The question-answer session continued after Kalyanam sat next to him on the floor too, and when he told Gandhiji that he was on leave to work in the ashram, Gandhiji wanted to know the salary he drew. He said, '250 rupees a month.' Gandhiji's immediate reaction was that of shock, 'Oh! I can only pay you sixty rupees a month.' To this, Kalyanam replied that he was willing to work for free! 'I didn't know why I said so. Perhaps I was so impressed with the simplicity of the man that I wanted to impress him. In any case, a strong work ethic mattered more to me than money, and I didn't go to the ashram expecting any salary. It was my passion for menial work that took me to the ashram.'

Bapu's last query was whether he knew to type, and the question surprised him. He wondered why he wanted to know his typing ability; after all, he had come to the ashram to do menial work and not to do any secretarial work. In fact, he hated office work so much that he literally ran away to the ashram. As it was mandatory for everybody who worked for the British to know typing, Kalyanam did know how to type. So he told Bapu that he could cope with some typing, still wondering why the Mahatma asked him about typing.

Kalyanam did not know at the time that Mahadev Desai, Mahatma Gandhi's long-time private secretary who took care of his every need, had died in prison in 1942. So he did not realise that he had put himself into consideration for the role of Gandhiji's stenographer from the moment he'd mentioned his fluency in English and Hindi.

After a while, all of them went back to the hotel, and started their journey back to the Sevagram Ashram the very next day. They were told that Bapu would arrive at the ashram later, after taking nature cure treatment at Panchgani and a couple of other places.

Kalyanam was still oblivious to the fact that Gandhiji would use him as his amanuensis. He would have laughed if someone had told him that. But life often takes surprising turns. Take Kalyanam's life, for instance. He was a former supporter of the British Raj who found himself involved in the anti-British Quit India movement. Soon, he had foregone the British way of life for the austerities of the Sevagram Ashram, and a few months on, he was the Mahatma's stenographer and again, a few months later, his personal secretary.

A life of sacrifice is the pinnacle of art, and is full of true joy. God accepts the sacrifice of the pure in heart. The willing sacrifice of the innocent is the most powerful retort to insolent tyranny that has yet been conceived by God or man.

—Mahatma Gandhi

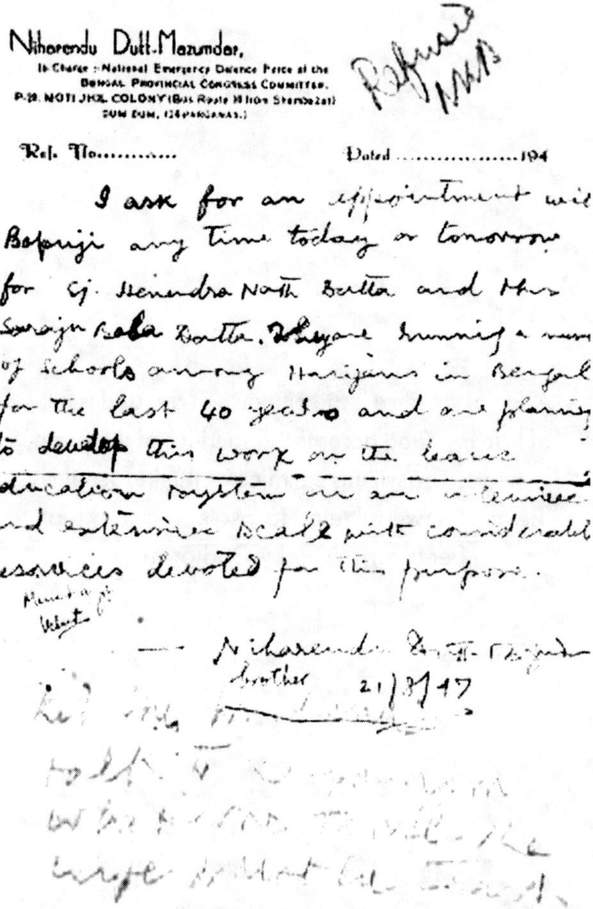

Niharendu Dutt-Mazumdar,
In Charge: National Emergency Defence Force of the Bengal Provincial Congress Committee.
P-20, Moti Jhil Colony
Dum Dum, (24 Parganas.)

Ref. No............ Dated..................194

I ask for an appointment with Bapuji any time today or tomorrow for Sj. Hemendra Nath Datta and Mrs Sarojini Bala Datta. They are running a number of schools among Harijans in Bengal for the last 40 years and are planning to develop this work on the basic education system on an intensive and extensive scale with considerable resources devoted for the purpose.

— Niharendu Dutt-Mazumdar
21/3/47

Niharendu Dutt Majumdar asks for an appointment with Bapu and Bapu writes, 'Talk to Kalyanam who knows Tamil….'

Personal Secretary to Mahatma 1944

It was only after a year or two of living in his first hut at Sevagram, called Adi Nivas, that Gandhiji moved to another hut. This hut is today known as the Bapu Kutir. The hut occupied by Kasturba is now called Ba Kutir. Bapu Kutir was originally prepared by Mirabehn for her own use, and was where she taught the villagers to hand-spin their own clothes. Once it was Bapu's, it became the place that national and international leaders came to, to meet him. Many decisions that affected India's destiny were taken there.In his hut, Gandhiji had hung two quotations that had had a major influence on him. The first was from John Ruskin's book 'Unto this Last' and read, 'The essence of lying is in deception, and not in words. A lie may be told by silence, by equivocation, by the accent on a syllable, by the glance of the eye attaching particular significance to a sentence and all these kinds of lies are worse and baser by many degrees than a lie plainly worded.' The second was from GC Larimer: When you are in the right, you can afford to keep your temper, and when you are in the wrong, you can't afford to lose it .

The day that all of the inmates of the Sevagram Ashram were waiting for finally arrived. The 1st of October1944. Mahatma Gandhi was coming back to the ashram after more than two years away in jail and treatment. Three people from the ashram went to the Wardha station to pick him up while the others waited at the ashram itself. When the car carrying Gandhiji and the others reached the ashram, the inmates stood outside to welcome him. Each of them prostrated themselves at his feet in turn. He blessed all of them with a smile on his tired face. He then went straight to his own hut, which had been kept closed during the period of his absence. They'd cleaned it thoroughly the day before his arrival, and like all the other huts, this one too had no locks.

Bapu had been away for two years, and there was a lot he had to catch up on. He called each one of the inmates separately to his room and enquired about their life during his absence. He wanted to know whether the British had troubled them in any way, and he was happy to hear that life was peaceful at the ashram.

Kalyanam's job as the Mahatma's new stenographer began the very next day. 'Till he came, I was working in the garden and the fields most of the time. Then the office manager started using me for some work in the office. My simple life changed dramatically upon Bapu's return to the ashram. Instead of working in the garden or the fields, I was doing his office work all the time. Initially, my job was only to type his letters but soon, I was taking care of most of his official work.'

As Kalyanam became an integral part of Bapu's life, he also got familiar with Bapu's daily routine in no time.

Bapu got up quite early; he was up and about by four in the morning. Kalyanam, then a young twenty-two, often wondered why he did so. But today, at the age of ninety-three, he understands why. 'Now I know that nobody past the age of seventy-five sleeps past 3 o'clock. Looking back at it, Gandhiji's early awakenings were nothing unusual, though I certainly didn't think so at the time.'

The first thing Bapu did on waking up was go to the toilet. After the jail term, he was too old and weak to walk to the toilet, and he needed to urinate quite often during the day, so the ashram people had fitted a commode for him that they took turns cleaning.

Austerity was evident in the way he washed his face too; he just took a little bit of water from the bottle kept near him and washed his face into a bowl so that not a single drop of water was wasted.

At 4.30 am, all the twenty inmates of the ashram assembled in his room for the morning prayers. Everybody was expected to attend the prayer meeting. 'If someone didn't attend the prayer, Bapu would come to know of it and didn't like it a bit. He believed that everybody's day should start with prayer. But he never scolded anyone, as he considered scolding a violent reaction. He was against all kinds of violence. So he indirectly asked one of us to inform the person that it would be better if he left the ashram.' While the inmates sang prayers from all religions, Bapu sat silently with his eyes closed.

After that, he had his morning drink of hot water with lemon and honey. Kalyanam still remembers that, 'he preferred his drink very hot and never used brass or silver tumblers—only white marble ones. As the drink was so hot, he used a small napkin to hold it to drink. He took at least ten minutes to finish drinking it, sipping away slowly at it until the tumbler was empty.' Not a drop of drink was wasted; it was expected of a man who didn't encourage wasting even a drop of water!

Though he was only seventy-five, Bapu was very weak after his illness. 'He looked much older than seventy-five. He always used a wooden spoon that he held with trembling hands to eat his meals', Kalyanam says.

After this, it was time to dictate letters. The day after he arrived, Bapu called Kalyanam to his room and asked, 'What languages do you speak?'

'I told him I knew Tamil, English and Hindi. He then told me that he wished to dictate a few letters in English. He said, "They have to be typed after that." I told him that I only knew to type in English. But he was fine with it. He then asked me to bring all the letters in English that had come to him', Kalyanam recollects that first day. He first brought twenty letters from the pile of thousands of letters he had tied in various bundles, segregated according to the language in which they were written. In the two years he was away in jail, nearly three thousand letters had come from all parts of the world and Bapu was very particular that he replied to each and every one of them.

How Bapu and he worked was, 'I would give him a letter to read, and then he would say something as a reply for me to write down. After that, he would give the letter back to me to note the return address down. I would go to my room, type it, and give it to him to correct', Kalyanam explains.

In the beginning, Kalyanam used to make a lot of mistakes in the drafts. 'That was because I couldn't decipher what he said with and without his dentures, but he corrected the mistakes in the draft. He never got angry with me for the mistakes I made. But if he was happy with my work, he always said, "Good!"'

This was done for an hour from 5 am to 6 am on every day of the week except Mondays. Gandhiji observed a vow of silence on Mondays. From six in the morning to six in the evening, he wouldn't speak to anybody. 'On Mondays, he would write down what he wished to convey on pieces of paper and pass them on to me. His writing was harder to understand than his speech. I made more mistakes than usual on Mondays, as I just couldn't read his handwriting! But he was very patient with me. He just corrected them silently, without even looking at me.'

As Kalyanam knew Tamil, he translated the Tamil letters for Bapu's benefit while Rajkumari Amrit Kaur (a linguist who later went on to become independent India's first Minister of Health) translated letters in German, French and other European languages. A Bengali girl translated letters written in Bengali.

After the letter-writing session, Bapu went for his morning walk all around the ashram compound with his hands on the shoulders of his two grand-nieces, Manu and Abha. This was something he never missed. If it were raining, he'd walk the same distance indoors. 'Though he was only seventy-five, he couldn't walk alone at all; he needed support at all times. The many fasts he had undertaken had affected his health. It was as he walked that he gave interviews to the press, answering the questions put to him as he walked. The journalists walked along with him and asked questions and he answered them in his feeble voice.'

Kalyanam also walked with them as it was his duty to note down whatever Bapu said in the interviews. These were then used in *Harijan*, the magazine that Bapu edited.

Generally the morning walk lasted about 40-45 minutes. After that, it was time for an oil massage and a bath. Bapu would lie down on a cot while somebody gave him a hot mustard oil massage. 'When the massage was given to him, Bapu invariably fell asleep, and went on sleeping for about half-an-hour after that. It was the girls or the doctor who attended to him, who usually massaged him. If they were otherwise occupied, the job fell on somebody else. It all depended on who was free at the time. He had his bath only after he'd woken up from his slumber. One thing he was particular about was hot water for bathing. Even on the hottest day, he bathed in hot water. However, he was very economical with his use of soap. He just rubbed himself with a towel while drying his body', Kalyanam remembers.

After the hot water bath, Bapu had his very simple meal of goat's milk and khakhra. The boiled vegetables used with khakhra were the cheapest available. That was because he was of the opinion that he should deny himself vegetables such as beans, carrots and cauliflowers that were inaccessible to India's poor. He also abstained from taking salt with his food for reasons well known to every Indian.

There is a story behind Bapu consuming only goat's milk. Once, when he was told that the milkman tortured cows and buffaloes for getting more milk, he took a vow that he would stop taking milk and milk products. It continued for nearly six years but when a severe attack of dysentery made him extremely weak and he was reduced to a skeleton, the doctors attending to him advised him to drink milk. But he refused to break his vow. He was persuaded to compromise on this and drink goat milk, as his vow pertained only to cow and buffalo milk.

After his meal, Bapu would begin to write; he wrote articles in English, Hindi and Gujarati. Not a moment was spent idle. 'He used the blank side of unwanted letters and envelopes that were slit open carefully. All these were converted into writing pads of different sizes.'

Kalyanam recalls that he never saw Bapu read any books at all. 'All his knowledge was from what he had read in his school and college days. He had an amazing memory and remembered every minute detail of every book he had ever read.'

He didn't read the daily newspaper either; it was Kalyanam's duty to tell him all the news after going through the morning papers. 'I had to read the papers first and then type the important bits on a piece of paper and place it before him. It was up to me to decide what he would consider important.'

'For example, if there was a news item about Rajendra Prasad (Independent India's first President) visiting Delhi, I would mention it in the précis I prepared for him. Sometimes, if a particular news item interested him, he would ask me to read out the entire report from the newspaper. He would also sometimes ask supplementary questions on reports he'd read—suppose I'd said that Rajendra Prasad had come back from a meeting, he would ask, "What did he say at the meeting?" He would then ask me to read the report in full from the newspaper.'

After catching up on the day's news, all of them had orange juice, as they were close to Nagpur (a city famous for its oranges).

Then Bapu would spin his loom for a half-hour. By then, the girls would have readied the mudpack to be applied on his stomach. Kalyanam remembers Bapu saying that, 'It was to remove all the impurities from one's body that the mudpack is applied to one's stomach.' Bapu would lie down and fall asleep for about half-an-hour, after which the girls would take it off him.

Five o'clock in the evening was the time for prayers with the general public on the ashram grounds. Before the prayer, Gandhiji would consume in his hut the same simple meal he'd had in the morning. Kalyanam still remembers those prayer meetings. 'Lots of people came to attend the prayer meetings where he spoke to the public about his plans for the country. He also told people about his talks with the British, if he'd had conversations with British delegations at the ashram. He would also tell people about ordinary matters like how to keep their surroundings clean and remain non-violent. Cleanliness was an obsession with him, so also non-violence.'

Before going to bed, everybody was expected to write a diary. 'Almost everyone, including Bapu, maintained a daily diary of what we did and what we did not do every day. We were supposed to record in our diary, our various acts of omission and commission. If anyone felt that he had done some wrong during the day, he would record it, adding that he would not repeat it again. I follow this practice even today. He lived life as it should be lived and ought to be lived. I never saw him sit idle even for one moment. Neither did I ever see him read any books or refer to a dictionary. He was a master of the English language, and he also wrote in Gujarati and Hindi.'

'I never saw him lose his temper even when someone committed a serious mistake. He had his own way of administering admonishments. I still remember one Sunday at a prayer meeting in Delhi, Manu and Abha fell out of tune while singing and began to giggle and laugh. This hurt Bapu deeply. He felt, the girls did not understand the importance of prayers. When they apologised later, he told them it was his mistake that he did not bring them up well as they were under his care. He made them publicly apologised for their mistakes.' There were times he went on a fast for mistakes made by others in the ashram.

Kishorelal Mashruwala, Gandhiji's life-time associate, was the chief administrator of ashram affairs. Bapu's senior secretary, Pyarelal, assisted by Parashuram, used to be by Bapu's side always. In addition to taking dictation and reading the précis of newspapers out to him, Kalyanam's duties included accompanying him everywhere and noting every word he said, using his discretion to pick out the most important letters and newspaper articles of the day, replying to correspondence, scheduling interviews, preparing his English speeches, and coordinating with the press.

'It was a full-time job and there was little respite. Being a workaholic, I never felt tired, as everything I did was interesting. Though I did all that Bapu asked me to do, I was only a clerk compared to the great Mahadev Desai. 'He had been Bapu's all-in-all but I was just an inexperienced young man who first became Bapu's stenographer and slowly, started doing many other work for Bapu. I realised soon that I was in the vicinity of greatness. It is a matter of supreme pride for me to have been so closely associated with the greatest man of the century.'

In short, he was a part of Bapu's everyday life, from very early morning till the Mahatma went to bed at about 9 o'clock.

I would say that if the village perishes, India will perish too. India will be no more India. Her own mission in the world will get lost. The revival of the village is possible only when it is no more exploited. Industrialization on a mass scale will necessarily lead to passive or active exploitation of the villagers as the problems of competition and marketing come in. Therefore, we have to concentrate on the village being self-contained, manufacturing mainly for use. Provided this character of the village industry is maintained, there would be no objection to villagers using even the modern machines and tools that they can make and can afford to use. Only they should not be used as a means of exploitation of others.

—Mahatma Gandhi

On trains with the Mahatma 1945-1948

It all began on a train journey in South Africa. On 31 May 1893, Mohandas Karamchand Gandhi was going to Pretoria in a first class carriage. A white man objected to his presence in the first class carriage and ordered him to move to the van compartment at the end of the train. Gandhi objected to this arrogance and refused to budge. But when the train reached Pietermaritzburg, a stop along the way to Pretoria, he was thrown out of the train for his impudence. As he sat in the waiting room in the cold winter night, he took the decision to stay on in South Africa to fight racism against Indians. That was the beginning of a new struggle which the world had not seen before;

> non-violent satyagraha. Gandhiji came back to India after having managed to get the Indian Relief Act (1914) passed following his arrival at a compromise with the South African leader, Jan Christiaan Smuts. In January 1915, he returned to India, then ruled by the British, to a rousing welcome. Before plunging headlong into a new struggle to free India, Gandhiji decided to tour the country—mainly its villages—with 'his ears open and mouth shut' to learn the realities of rural life in India first hand. It was the trains that took him all around the country. Where the trains did not take him, he walked. In May 1915, Bapu settled down on the banks of the river Sabarmati in the outskirts of Ahmedabad and built an ashram known as the Sabarmati Ashram.

Train journeys were an integral and important part of Mahatma Gandhi's life. To understand India and its people and solve the country's problems, he travelled by train to each and every corner of India. As a personal assistant to the Mahatma, Kalyanam accompanied him on his many trips to different parts of India in his tours of Calcutta, East Bengal, Bihar, Kashmir, Shimla, Delhi and the entire south of India.

Gandhiji's entourage generally consisted of his senior secretary Pyarelal, his assistants Parshuram and Kalyanam and his two grand-nieces Manu and Abha. In addition, on some trips, his doctor, Sushila Nayyar, would accompany them too.

But on the first journey Kalyanam took with the Mahatma in the first week of December 1945, to Calcutta, the entourage was much smaller. It comprised only Kalyanam, Bapu's grand- nieces and another ashram inmate. Bapu was going to Calcutta to meet the famine-stricken people (the Great Bengal Famine) and study their problems. It was a journey Kalyanam could never forget for the shocks it gave him.

The first shock he had was the realisation that they were travelling third class. He had expected them to travel first class; after all they were travelling with Gandhiji; he was unaware of the fact that Gandhiji always travelled in a third class compartment. But the compartment they took was empty of any passengers save for Gandhiji and his entourage. Out of respect for Bapu, no other passenger entered the compartment.

'The British government used to place a full compartment at his disposal, for they respected him in spite of the fact that he fought against them', Kalyanam says, as he recalls the fairness of the British.

The next shock he had was when Bapu asked him whether he'd bought the tickets. But Kalyanam hadn't! 'This was the first time I was travelling with him. I was new to the ashram too. When Bapu asked me to go with him, I just went with him. I thought somebody else would have bought the tickets for all of us. When I was in service with the British government, whenever we had to travel, such as for instance when we moved from Delhi to Shimla for the summer, the Establishment Section of the office bought tickets for us. I assumed things worked the same way at the ashram.'

Gandhiji was a bit worried that he was travelling without tickets. The train's next stop was at Pune and when the train approached the Nagpur station, Bapu told Kalyanam to ask the Station Master to see him. As the train reached the station, Kalyanam prepared to step out, but he was unable to do so, thanks to the thousands of people who had assembled on the platform to have a darshan of Gandhiji.

Kalyanam remembers that whenever Bapu travelled, newspapers carried all the details of the places the train planned on stopping at, so that ordinary people could meet him there. At some places, he spoke to the assembled people if they requested him to. But he mostly just stood by the train door with folded hands or waved to them.

The moment Kalyanam spotted the Station Master among the jostling crowd, he squeezed past them and told him that Bapu wanted to talk to him. 'He was a little surprised at first. But he was soon elated that he was going to meet Gandhiji. He entered the compartment and did a pranam. Bapu said pointing to me, "This young fellow joined me recently, and he has not bought the tickets." The Station Master replied, "*Saab, aap ko kya zaroorat hain ticket lene ki. Aap itne bade aadmi hain* [Sir, there's no need for you to buy tickets. You're such a great man]." Bapu asked him, "Do you allow all great men to travel for free? If so, that is wrong! If you don't charge us for the tickets, I will report you to the railway officials and you will lose your job." The poor Station Master relented and agreed to sell us the tickets.'

Kalyanam paid for the tickets from his pocket and collected a voucher from the Station Master!

Another journey that surprised him took place on a Monday; the day Bapu observed silence. Instead of dictating as he did always, Bapu himself drafted a short letter to the Viceroy of India and handed it to Kalyanam for typing. What Kalyanam did not know was that the letter was to be delivered to Mridula Sarabhai at the Patna railway station, so that it could be posted to Lord Wavel, the Viceroy, immediately. As he had not taken his typewriter with him, Kalyanam thought he could type the draft once they reached Calcutta.

After Gandhi broke his silence at six in the evening, he asked Kalyanam who was sitting opposite him in the compartment, 'Kalyanam, where is the letter? Have you typed it?' A nervous Kalyanam replied that he hadn't yet as he didn't have his typewriter with him. It irritated the Mahatma so much that he muttered, 'When I send for a barber, I expect him to bring his tools.' Kalyanam just stood there unable to come out with any excuse. 'Normally, when people travel, they spend their time gossiping, playing cards, reading story books or dozing. This was the first time that I'd come across a person who did serious work on a train.'

Kalyanam then had two hours to get the letter ready before the train got to Patna. Manu and Abha told him that the adjoining compartment had a few journalists who were travelling with Gandhiji, and he could borrow a typewriter from one of them. Unfortunately, the typewriter was not in very good condition and had an old ribbon, and that made for a very poor draft. He thought the quality of the letter would make Bapu angrier still, but he signed the letter after making just one correction.

Another task Kalyanam, Bapu's grand-nieces, or whoever else happened to be travelling with the team, had to undertake was to get down with a collection bag at each of the stations where huge crowds had assembled. The money collected was used for the Harijan welfare fund; the money collected was never counted, the collection bags were just handed over to the bankers who came to collect it at the entourage's final stop.

On one occasion, the train they were travelling was running late, and hence had an unscheduled stop. As it was not publicised, there was no one at the station to see Bapu. When he noticed a chaiwala shouting *garam chai*, Bapu called him and ordered two trays of tea as there were three Europeans also travelling with Bapu.

The chaiwala came inside and placed the tray in front of him but did not recognise Bapu. The funny incident that happened then was between Kalyanam and Horace Alexander, the guest. 'I asked him whether I should make a cup of tea for him. He said, "No, we will make it ourselves. We need only a cup of tea while you people have a cup and saucer full of tea." He was referring to the Indian way of drinking tea from the saucer. On hearing his comment, Bapu burst out laughing.' According to Kalyanam, reaching Calcutta in 1946 with Bapu was also an unforgettable experience. 'Calcutta was rioting at the time and many Hindus were being killed. So Bapu went there to quell the riots. His intention was to meet all the parties involved."

In Calcutta, they stayed at the Sodepur Ashram run by Sathish Chandra Dasgupta for three days. 'Bapu spent all of his time meeting one delegation after another. First came a delegation of Muslims who complained that the Hindus were attacking and killing them. The moment they left, a Hindu delegation came and made the same complaint about the Muslims. This pattern repeated itself for days and nights on end; the Hindus complaining about Muslims, and the Muslims about the Hindus.'

As Gandhi was fully immersed in meeting delegation after delegation, he had no time to assign any work to Kalyanam; a terribly boring fate for somebody who was as much of a workaholic as Bapu himself. 'There were no dictations; he just talked and talked to people. Had we been in our ashram, I would have gone out and worked in the fields. But here, I had no idea as to what to do.'

As people always surrounded Gandhi, Kalyanam could not even ask Bapu for a solution to his dilemma. Eventually, he managed to get a few minutes of Bapu's time as he made his way back from the toilet. 'The toilet was along a corridor about thirty yards from his room. As he walked down the corridor, I caught hold of him and said, "Bapu, I am bored. You haven't asked me to do anything for the last two days. I have absolutely nothing to do." Bapu replied as he continued to walk, "How can you say that you have no work? There is enough work everywhere. I just had a bowel movement; go away and clean it."'

Without saying another word, Kalyanam went away and cleaned it up. 'What he said was true. We cannot say there is no work to do. He also taught me the dignity of labour. How could you expect him to waste time cleaning the toilet when there were bigger things to do like getting India's independence? I learnt the habit of cleaning from the British and it only got better after I joined Bapu. In fact, Bapu considered me the best cleaner.

'He used to tell the others, "Look at the way Kalyanam cleans everything." Once, after Sushila Nayyar opened a bottle of water and kept the cap on the floor with its lower portion touching the floor. When I saw this, I immediately kept it upside down so that no dirt went to the water when one closed the bottle. Bapu saw me doing this and told Sushila Nayyar, "see, Kalyanam is not a doctor but he knows what cleanliness is all about."' Kalyanam sounded proud as he recounted the compliment after all these years.

If India takes up the doctrine of the sword, she may gain momentary victory. Then India will cease to be the pride of my heart. I am wedded to India because I owe my all to her. I believe absolutely that she has a mission for the world. She is not to copy Europe blindly. India's acceptance of the doctrine of the sword will be the hour of my trial. I hope I shall not be found wanting. My religion has no geographical limits. If I have a living faith in it, it will transcend my love for India herself. My life is dedicated to service of India through the religion of non-violence. If India makes violence her creed, and I have survived, I would not care to live in India. She will cease to evoke any pride in me. My patriotism is subservient to my religion. I cling to India like a child to its mother's breast because I feel that she gives me the spiritual nourishment I need. She has the environment that responds to my highest aspirations. When that faith is gone, I shall feel like an orphan without hope of ever finding a guardian.

— Mahatma Gandhi

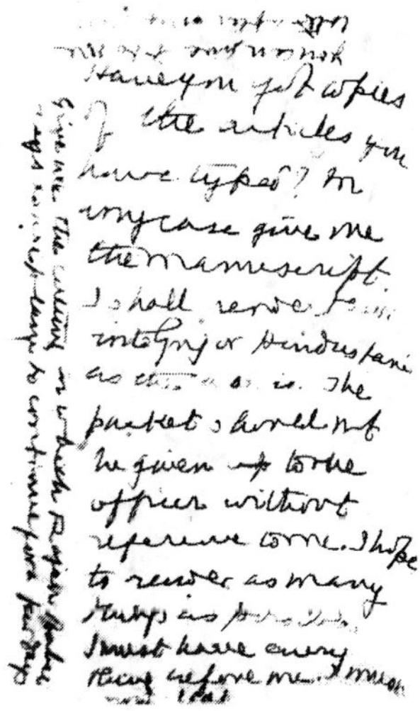

TRANSCRIPTION OF MAHATMA GANDHI'S
NOTE TO KALYANAM ON HIS SILENCE DAY

....

LATER AFTER MY SLEEP
YOU CAN GIVE IT TO ME
HAVE YOU GOT COPIES
OF THE ARTICLES YOU
HAVE TYPED ? IN
ANY CASE GIVE ME
THE MANUSCRIPT.
I SHALL RENDER THEM
INTO GUJ OR HINDUSTANI
AS THE CASE IS. THE
PACKET SHOULD NOT
BE GIVEN TO THE
OFFICER WITHOUT
REFERENCE TO ME. I HOPE
TO RENDER AS MANY
THINGS AS POSSIBLE.
I MUST HAVE EVERY
THING BEFORE ME. I MUST
NOW SLEEP.

GIVE ME THE CUTTING IN WHICH RAJEN BABU
SAYS TO KRIPALANI TO CONTINUE FOR A FEW DAYS.

Note written by Bapu to Kalyanam on the day he observed silence, and the typed version

From Sevagram to Bhangi Colony 1946-1947

The Gandhi family was very well known and respected in Rajkot. In this town, it was a Mahar [a Dalit caste] called Uka who did the scavenging. If the young Mohandas Gandhi ever touched Uka, his mother Putlibai forced him to bathe. Mohandas, who was otherwise a docile and obedient son, did not like it. The 12-year-old would argue with his mother saying, 'Uka serves us by cleaning dirt and filth, how can his touch pollute me? I shall not disobey you, but the Ramayana says that Rama embraced Guhaka, a chandal (a caste considered untouchable). The Ramayana cannot mislead us.' Putlibai had no answer to his argument. Later on, though he criticised

> many western customs, he admitted repeatedly that he learnt sanitation from the West. His desire was to introduce cleanliness of that sort to India. Once a foreigner asked Gandhi:'If you are made the Viceroy of India for a day, what would you do?' Gandhiji said:'I shall clean the Augean stables of the scavengers near the Viceroy's house.' The questioner continued, 'Supposing your term is extended by a day, then what would you do?' Gandhi answered, 'The very same work shall I do the next day.' Once when the villagers near his ashram refused to cover their excreta with earth and said, 'Surely, this is a Bhangi's (a low-caste cleaner's) work. It is sinful to look at faeces, more so to throw earth on it', an angry Gandhiji personally ensured that the excreta was covered To set an example, he often made his way to the villages with a bucket and a broom. The ashram dwellers, and even some of the guests, went with him with buckets full of mud to clean up the faeces. Gandhiji used to say in anguish, 'Look at the Bhangi as he eats; he is surrounded by filth. It is enough to break one's heart. That is why I say, everyone must be his own scavenger.'

Following the release from jail of himself and the other Congress leaders, Bapu started holding multiple meetings with British delegations and Congress leaders at the Sevagran Ashram. Congress Working Committee meetings during the period were also held there.

While the discussions went on for days, some of the leaders—including the members of the British delegation—stayed at the ashram. Among the leaders who spent a long time at the Ashram was Khan Abdul Ghaffar Khan, who was very close to Bapu. Khan spent so much time at the ashram that he was allocated his own hut.

Kalyanam remembers one visit that Ghaffar Khan made to the ashram with his young son very clearly indeed. 'As I said before, the food at Sevagram was very simple and exclusively vegetarian. Khan's son, however, was used to eating meat. He ate the simple food without any complaint on the first day, and then continued to do so with great difficulty on the second day. On the third day, his patience gave away and he complained to his father, "Do they not serve any meat here? I am tired of this food."

'When Bapu asked him whether he was comfortable at the ashram, the boy quite frankly told him, "I don't like the food, especially the same kaddu (pumpkin) everyday." Bapu laughed and asked the boy what it was he wanted. He said, "Murgi (chicken)." Bapu immediately asked me to arrange for a chicken to feed the boy. But Abdul Ghaffar Khan put a stop to that, "Bapu, he should learn to eat the food that is available. He should eat the ashram food when he is here. Tomorrow, when we are back in Kabul, he can have his murgi!" He did not let Bapu serve him any non-vegetarian food at the ashram.'

Kalyanam went on to add, 'This shows how accommodating Bapu could be. He was a vegetarian and never allowed anyone to have meat at his ashram. But he was acutely aware of his responsibility as a host to make his atithis (guests) comfortable, even if they were but small boys!'

Abdul Ghaffar Khan was a very close friend of Bapu and both of them sat for hours talking about the British, Hindu-Muslim unity and independence. 'He considered Bapu to be too great a man to dare sit down next to him as they talked. He respected Bapu a lot and always listened to everything he had to say.'

In the following years, after Gandhiji and his acolytes had moved to the Bhangi Colony in Delhi, Abdul Ghaffar Khan remained a regular visitor, especially during the course of discussions on independence and partition. Once, after meeting Bapu, he had to meet Muhammad Ali Jinnah. He took Kalyanam with him, as he was not familiar with the streets of Delhi. At the meeting, Kalyanam listened quietly as Jinnah spoke of the North-West Frontier Province's (now Khyber Pakhtunkhwa, in Pakistan) place in a post-independence settlement.

'Jinnah wanted the North-West Frontier Province to join Pakistan. Khan listened to him, though he was set against the idea of partitioning India. The next day, however, the newspapers carried statements from Jinnah that completely misrepresented Khan's position on the creation of Pakistan. In the morning when he saw the papers, Khan was shocked. He looked at me and said, "You were with me. Did you hear me say anything of this sort? I didn't support him at all. He lies!" He felt so embarrassed that he went to Bapu and said, "I didn't say all these things." Bapu then helped him write a letter in English to Jinnah [Khan couldn't write in English] to set the record straight.'

C Rajagopalachari, who later went on to become the first Indian Governor-General of India and was fondly known as Rajaji, was another regular visitor to the ashram. In addition to the ties of friendship that bound him and Bapu together, they were related by marriage—Gandhiji's son Devdas Gandhi was married to Rajaji's daughter. 'But both of them never behaved like they were related. Neither did the other a favour that they wouldn't do another.'

Rajaji was a scholar and a man of great intelligence. Bapu had great respect for him, and that was why Bapu described him as his 'conscience keeper'. Rajaji didn't participate in the Quit India Resolution, as he was against it. Only he had the courage to go against the ideals of Gandhiji.

As Bapu preferred to sit cross-legged on the floor, everybody who came to see him followed suit. 'The only person who used the chair in front of Bapu was Sir M Visvesvaraya (one of India's greatest engineers, later awarded the Bharat Ratna in 1955). He had trouble with his back. All of the rest, be they foreign delegations or Lord Mountbatten (the Viceroy of India from February to August 1947, and the Governor General of India from August 1947 to June 1948) and his wife (who visited quite often), all sat on the floor out of respect for Gandhiji. Even when we offered them chairs, they refused.'

A third regular visitor was Jawaharlal Nehru who came both alone and with other Congressmen to see Bapu. In no time, Kalyanam realised that 'this very handsome man' was Bapu's favourite. 'Nehru never stayed at the ashram but had food there many a times. Though he was used to better food than the fare at the ashram, he ate the same simple food we ate and used the same toilets we did. He never kicked up a fuss about it.'

Bapu often described the ashram as a lunatic asylum as all kinds of people came and settled down there. 'Once, a European came with his teenage son to stay for a week. Bapu asked me to take care of his needs. On the first day, when I asked them to come for lunch, the father said, "we do not eat anything except boiled potatoes and drink nothing but water." I had to, therefore, arrange boiled potatoes and water for them!'

Kalyanam had the opportunity to meet all the important Congress leaders when he stayed with Bapu as the Congress Working Committee meetings were held at the Sevagram Ashram. 'I was attached to Bapu, and I was his man. But when the other leaders visited him, I took care of them too. They would ask me to do little things like getting them water or bringing them stationery. Though I was always present, I had nothing to do with what was discussed in the talks. They spoke about the strategies they had to adopt to send the British back and things like that. But I never took any interest in that.'

From April 1946 on, Bapu and his team were constantly travelling to Delhi to meet the British Cabinet Mission, and Bapu's talks with them on creating a Constitution for Independent India went on till the end of June. Though Kalyanam was witness to the flurry of activity, nobody from Bapu's team was allowed to be present when the discussions happened.

Though they went back to Sevagram in July 1946, they had to leave almost immediately afterwards, as Bapu was convinced by the leadership of the Congress Party to move to Delhi in order to be closer to the centre of all of the frenetic discussions about the future of India. He, therefore, took up residence in Delhi on the 25th of August. This move was a signal to the residents of the ashram that India's day of freedom was near indeed.

'On the eve of our departure for Delhi, at the prayer meeting, Bapu told all those who had assembled, "I am not sure when I will be able to return from Delhi..." And how prophetic his words turned out to be! We never came back to Sevagram', Kalyanam recalls.

Usually, when Bapu visited Bombay or Delhi, he stayed at Birla House as a guest of industrialist GD Birla. But this time around, he knew he was going to have to stay for a much longer period, and therefore expressed his desire to live with the Harijans (Dalits). In response to the request, Birla built a row of temporary sheds in an open space close to where the sweepers lived, called Bhangi Colony.

During this time, in addition to his usual duties, Kalyanam had to ferry the articles Gandhiji had written for the *Harijan* magazine every Monday to the Willingdon Airport (now known as the Safdarjung airport), from where they were ferried to Ahmedabad for free by Air India. The problem Kalyanam faced, however, was that the airport was a fair distance away from where they lived. Though Birla had placed a car at Bapu's disposal, the others never used it. So, Kalyanam had to make an arduous three-hour-long journey by bus to the airport.

Bapu understood that Kalyanam was not there for him for hours because of the long travel. So, one day, Bapu told Rajendra Prasad, who lived near the airport and visited Gandhiji every morning at five, 'Please take Kalyanam to the airport so that he can save some time.'

'I still remember the date; it was on the 3rd of June 1947. From that day on, I went with Rajendra Babu, in his car to the airport every Monday. His driver would first drop him off at his house and then drop me at the airport. Though I had to take a bus back, it saved a lot of time. This arrangement continued even after India had gained her freedom and Rajendra Babu was appointed the Food Minister of the country.'

As discussions on India's independence, its partition, and solutions to the problem of the Princely States continued, one day Gandhiji decided to leave Delhi for Kashmir. Kalyanam could not understand why at the time, though.

Upon hearing of the trip, Jawaharlal Nehru, who hailed from Kashmir, wanted Bapu to do some sightseeing. He even came to Bhangi Colony and told Bapu of some places to visit. 'However', Kalyanam recalls with a chuckle, 'Bapu had only one hobby. Work, and then more work. He never found the time to go sightseeing, and he also denied those of us who were anxious to see new places, the opportunity to see them.'

In addition, Nehru imposed one condition on Gandhiji's trip. As Kashmir was a Princely State at the time, and her Hindu ruler, who presided over a majority Muslim population, was struggling to decide between independence and accession to either India or Pakistan, Nehru insisted that Bapu not hold any rallies or talk politics when there. Bapu acquiesced.

They left Delhi by train on the night of 30 July 1947 and reached Kashmir on the evening of the first. 'We were put up in the palatial bungalow of Kishorilal Sethi, a well-known local contractor. When the word spread that Bapu was in the palace, people from the neighbouring villages came to see him. Most of them wanted the King to release Sheikh Abdullah from jail, and requested that Bapu intervene. But he declined to do so, saying he had not come on a political mission.'

When people asked him whether Kashmir should join India or Pakistan, he replied, 'Let the people of Kashmir decide.' That was when Kalyanam understood the intention behind Bapu's sudden visit to Kashmir; Bapu wished to know the minds of the people of Kashmir.

On the morning of the 4th, they went to Jammu, and from there down to Rawalpindi in what is now Pakistan. In Rawalpindi, Bapu visited the Wah Refugee Camp, which held around ten thousand Hindu refugees.

'Several thousand had left the camp for fear of being killed by Muslims, or being forced to convert to Islam if they wished to continue to stay in west Punjab. The tension in the atmosphere there was palpable', Kalyanam recounts.

After the visit, Bapu and his entourage made their way back to the Bhangi Colony in Delhi, where they remained until a few days before India's independence.

I learnt thirty-five years ago that a lavatory must be as clean as a drawingroom. I learnt this in the West. I believe that many rules about cleanliness in lavatories are observed more scrupulously in the West than in the East. The cause of many of our diseases is the condition of our lavatories and our bad habit of disposing of excreta anywhere and everywhere. I, therefore, believe in the absolute necessity of a clean place for answering the call of nature and clean articles for use at the time. I have accustomed myself to them and wish that all others should do the same. The habit has become so firm in me that even if I wished to change it, I would not be able to do so. Nor do I wish to change it. If you become your own scavengers, you will make your surroundings clean. It needs no less courage to become an expert scavenger than to win a Victoria Cross.

—Mahatma Gandhi

The Failure to stop Partition 1946-1947

The small district of Noakhali (now in Bangladesh) is intimately connected with the story of India's independence. The Hindu-Muslim riots that started in Noakhali towards the end of 1946 turned into a genocide of the Hindus and carnage that heralded India's independence. Thousands upon thousands of people lost their lives and in Muslim dominated areas, Hindus were massacred. It hurt Bapu personally, as he had spent the preceding decades preaching Ahmisa (non-violence) to people. He decided to head to Noakhali. He said at the time, 'I do not know what I shall be able to do there. All I know is that I won't be at peace with myself unless I go.... One

> active thought, proceeding from its depths in its nascent purity and endowed with all the undivided intensity of one's being, can become dynamic and make history.' 'The more I go about these parts, the more I find that your worst enemy is fear. The terrorist as well as the terrorised is equally its victim. It eats into their vitals. The former fears something in his victim. It may be the latter's religion, which is different from the terrorist's, or the latter's riches. But there has never been and never will be a man who can intimidate one who has cast out fear from his heart because God is always by the side of the fearless. If we make God our sole refuge, all our fears will vanish. Unless you cultivate fearlessness there will never be any peace in these parts for Hindus or for Muslims', Gandhi prophesied.

On 12 August 1946, when the Viceroy asked Nehru to form an interim government, Jinnah declared a 'Direct Action Day' in Bengal and the result was bloodshed in many places in India. In short, Jinnah wanted nothing but the partition of India and was willing to stop at nothing in order to achieve his mission.

Jinnah was the only leader who never visited Bapu at the ashram. It was always Bapu who went to meet him. Though a silent spectator to what was happening around him, Kalyanam understood quite clearly that, 'Jinnah did not trust the Hindu majority population to give the Muslim community a fair deal due to the humiliation he had been subject to by Pundit Nehru and the other Hindu leaders. It was this distrust that gave birth to the Muslim League under Jinnah's leadership. The sole aim of the League was to have a separate state for the Muslims and prevent them being dominated by the Hindu majority. Jinnah was adamant about getting a separate state for Pakistan and it saddened Bapu immensely.'

From what he had observed and heard, Kalyanam was of the opinion that 'though Jinnah was once a nationalist and a Congressman, Nehru never treated him properly. He was a very senior lawyer, but Nehru didn't give him due respect. That was why there was this animosity between the two of them.'

For example, in 1937 [after the Indian provincial elections], Congressmen were asked to form a government by the British [after having won 707 of the 1,585 seats]. Though the Muslim League obtained a fair number of seats [106], Nehru insisted that the Muslims who had won on Muslim League tickets become Congressmen. The rift began then, and the Ministry was formed without them. The enmity between Nehru and Jinnah also dates back to this point.

Perhaps it is the trouble Jinnah gave Bapu personally, and the fact that he was witness to the traumatic partition of India, that makes Kalyanam look at Jinnah quite critically today. He recalls, 'Jinnah was not a devout Muslim. We all knew that he consumed alcohol and ate pork, both of which are un-Islamic acts. He seldom visited the mosque. He knew very little Urdu and no Arabic at all. It was well known that when in his forties, he went out of his religion to marry a Parsi girl. That said, however, when his only daughter married a Parsi-turned-Christian, he disowned her.'

Gandhiji had expressed in his articles and speeches his unhappiness and frustration at being unable to convince Jinnah to not go ahead with the idea of partition. Kalyanam transcribed many letters dictated by Bapu to Jinnah, assuring him that Muslims would be treated well in an independent India and that he should drop the idea of a separate country.

'He wrote several letters and spoke to Jinnah in person several times. Bapu was so distraught in those days that he went to the extent of telling Jinnah that he would give him the whole of India so that he could become the Prime Minister.'

It surprised Kalyanam then that Nehru and Patel, the two main leaders who worked hard in the political discussions, could not anticipate the blood and tears that would follow partition. 'I felt they thought it would be a smooth process. Partition could never be painless and without tears. They truly believed that once the country was divided, everything would be alright. It was their biggest mistake.'

But Bapu had the premonition that 'partition would lead to endless distrust', which continues even today.

While talks between the British and the Congress, and the Congress and Jinnah's Muslim League went on, Hindus and Muslims were killing each other in faraway Noakhali. Pained by this news, Gandhiji decided to go there to pacify the people. Thus, from 7 November 1946 to 2 March 1947, he lived and suffered with the people, and tried to bring peace in Noakhali.

As Kalyanam accompanied Gandhiji wherever he went, he was with Bapu at Noakhali too. 'Everyday, we would go to places where people fought each other, stand amidst them and try to pacify them with sweet words. Bapu told the Muslims who wanted Pakistan that they would be safe staying with the Hindus and that nothing would happen to them in India. This went on for many days. But he was eventually successful; gradually, the fighting came to an end.'

After achieving some success in Naokhali, Bapu went to Bihar and tried the same thing there too. 'We went from village to village, mostly on foot, asking people to remain calm. Unlike in Noakhali where we had to face a lot of hostility, he was surrounded by supportive crowds in Bihar. We collected money for injured and homeless Muslims. Many women gave away their jewellery. He told the people, "If you ever become mad again, you must destroy me first." His words had an impact on them as they showered a lot of love on him.'

In May 1947, he was called to Delhi. The new Viceroy, Lord Mountbatten, had succeeded in persuading the Congress leaders to accept Jinnah's insistent demand for the partition of India as a condition precedent for British withdrawal.

Gandhiji was against partition at any cost, but he was unable to convince the Congress leaders of the wisdom of his stand.

Bapu could stop the Hindu-Muslim fights for a while, but none of his entreaties had any effect on Jinnah. He was adamant about partitioning India. While Lord Mountbatten, Khan Abdul Ghaffar Khan and Maulana Azad welcomed the idea of Jinnah becoming the Prime Minister of India, Nehru and the Hindu majority in the AICC rejected the proposal outright.

Maulana Azad went to the extent of suggesting that the demand for Independence itself be deferred till there was unity of hearts, if only to avoid partition. Gandhiji said, 'Partition could have been avoided had the non-Muslim population paid heed to my advice. They have deserted me and let me down.'

A heartbroken Gandhi and his retinue went to Calcutta when everybody else in the Indian National Congress agreed to divide the country.

What happened behind Gandhiji's back still angers Kalyanam. 'The others planned everything without involving him, though he had been a part of all the discussions and dialogues until then. He was absolutely against the division of India till his last breath. He couldn't fathom the idea of dividing India, which was a single entity under the Mughal and the British, into Hindustan and Pakistan. He had not the slightest doubt that division of the country would be a great blunder. He always said, "You can have Pakistan only over my dead body."'

'But he couldn't do anything; he was just a helpless onlooker as the horrific events of partition unfolded. When he came to know that the country would be divided, he didn't say anything; he just kept quiet. He was sad that they (the Congress leaders) had agreed to the partition. That was how Pakistan was created — over Bapu's tears.'

Kalyanam still has one question in his mind. 'Bapu had undertaken so many fasts unto death in his life to achieve his ideals. But somehow, in spite of the great distress at the prospect of his country being divided, his inner voice did not call upon him to fast for this. Would history have been different if this man of God had challenged the partition of India with this weapon? Perhaps, he knew that even this weapon would not have worked under the circumstances.'

Hindu -Muslim unity can be established only through peace. I know it is a difficult task. Our non-violence is tested when we can remain calm even though a volcano may be raging in our hearts. And what is the harm if all of us die by remaining peaceful? Even if some Muslim kills me, he will be after all my brother. If we fail to preserve peace and forcibly retain the country's unity our hearts will remain divided. And, if [the spirit of] Pakistan persists in our hearts and we are not willing on any account to live with our brothers peacefully, I warn you India will not be able to retain her freedom. Yes, in a way, Pakistan can be full of the nectar of nectar. But why do you need pistols, spears and swords for it? A Pakistan forced on others will be full of poison. Why should we force people to swallow this poison? If I do not poison others' hearts, have no poison in mine

> and do not mind it if I have to die fighting all others, the Pakistan [thus achieved] would be a thing of love and so would be India. India will be full of the nectar of love when she belongs not only to the Hindus but also to the Muslims, Parsis, Christians and Sikhs in equal measure. And that Pakistan alone would be full of love where there would be place for all the communities and no malice against anyone. Because I am a believer in such an India and such a Pakistan, I would recite Auz-o-Billahi even while I recite the Gayatri and the Gita. Probably no one is more distressed than I am over the impending division of India. But I have no desire to launch a struggle against what promises to be an accomplished fact. We shall tear ourselves asunder in the womb of the mother who bear us.
>
> —Mahatma Gandhi

Independence Day

15 August 1947

On the midnight of the 15th of August 1947, Jawaharlal Nehru, the first Prime Minister of a new country, delivered a memorable speech, The Tryst with Destiny. 'Long years ago we made a tryst with destiny, and now the time comes when we shall redeem our pledge, not wholly or in full measure, but very substantially. At the stroke of the midnight hour, when the world sleeps, India will awake to life and freedom. A moment comes, which comes but rarely in history, when we step out from the old to the new, when an age ends, and when the soul of a nation, long suppressed, finds utterance. The achievement we celebrate today is but a step, an opening of opportunity, to the

> greater triumphs and achievements that await us. Are we brave enough and wise enough to grasp this opportunity and accept the challenge of the future? Freedom and power bring responsibility. The responsibility rests upon this assembly, a sovereign body representing the sovereign people of India. Before the birth of freedom we have endured all the pains of labour and our hearts are heavy with the memory of this sorrow. Some of those pains continue even now. Nevertheless, the past is over and it is the future that beckons to us now. The ambition of the greatest man of our generation has been to wipe every tear from every eye. That may be beyond us, but as long as there are tears and suffering, so long our work will not be over.'

Nehru invited 'the greatest man of the generation', Bapu, to the historic Independence night event. Lord Mountbatten sent him a wire. But Bapu refused to go to Delhi. In response to their requests, he said, 'I will not come. My job is here, to bring about unity between the Hindus and the Muslims. Independence is not so important for me. What is the purpose of independence when people can't live together and fight amongst themselves and kill each other?'

There were other senior leaders too who felt like Bapu. Rajaji's reaction to the Independence celebrations was, 'We got independence long before we were worthy of it.' Rajaji had felt that fixing 15 August 1947 for the transfer of power to Indians was not realistic. People like him were of the opinion that having decided to divide the country, this date should have been suitably extended so as to permit the exchange of population in a peaceful manner and merger of the Princely States with one dominion or the other.

It is a matter of conjuncture how the fate of India would have changed, had the country not been divided into two, and that too in such a tearing hurry? A lot of animosity was created between Hindus, Muslims and Sikhs because of the creation of a new state on the basis of religion. Lakhs of families having their moorings on either side for centuries were forced to migrate overnight from one country to another for no fault of theirs. This resulted in people fleeing for safety, risking their lives and leaving behind their entire life's savings.

Kalyanam feels, 'The resultant killings, abduction, loot, arson and misery could have been avoided. Kashmir would have remained intact, and the peace and tranquillity that prevailed during the British rule could have continued. What is more, Bapu's life could have been saved.'

Kalyanam, who was with Bapu while the history of a new country was being written, says, 'We were in Beliaghata, Calcutta, which saw a lot of internecine bloodshed in the days immediately preceding independence. We were stationed in a house called the Haidari Mansion, owned by a Muslim woman. Because the Hindus and Muslims were fighting, Bapu wanted to stay in a Muslim's house. It was a big, dilapidated bungalow with all of the doors and windows broken. We were given one room, where all of us slept. There was only one latrine too, which we shared with the other volunteers and the local policemen. We had to struggle to get the place into a state fit for human habitation.'

It was with this violence as the backdrop that the 15th of August 1947 dawned. Everybody in India rejoiced; everybody except for the one man who had relentlessly fought for India's freedom through all of the preceding years. When people distributed sweets celebrating India's independence, he lay on a mattress with his eyes closed.

Independence brought a brief respite to the denizens of Beliaghata. The violence stopped temporarily on the day, though it resumed with renewed ferocity in the days that followed.

Did the dawn of independence at least bring about the birth of a nation of the sort Bapu desired? Sadly, the answer to that question is no. Bapu wished for an India 'with a Prime Minister who will continue to live in his hut, sleep in the open and not occupy any bungalow allotted by the government. Since he will not have any knowledge of English, Nehru should act as his Private Secretary and attend to all of the secretarial work on his behalf. Nehru will also meet the ambassadors and other high dignitaries coming from abroad and hold talks with them.'

On the 20th of August, while addressing the people in his post-prayer meeting in Beliaghata, Bapu spoke about India's national flag. He said that both India and Pakistan should display each other's flags prominently, for the sake of good relations between the two countries. But that statement didn't go down well with the people at all—a fact presumably not surprising given the torrents of blood that had been shed in the preceding months for the sake of the division of the country.

When the fighting and killings continued unabated despite Bapu's several appeals, a hurt Mahatma Gandhi used the last weapon in his arsenal: to go on a fast.

The fast started on the 31st of August in Beliaghata. However, even as he fasted, he continued to work every day as he normally did until such time as his frail and tired body could take it no more. Whenever that happened, he would lie down, unable to speak, and continue to write letters in his trembling hand. Kalyanam remembers that after a few days of this, he was so exhausted as to not be able to lift a finger.

As he fasted, some people felt very angry with Bapu, and felt that he was taking the side of one community over the other. Thus it came to pass that an angry mob began to throw stones at the house they lived in. Fortunately, nobody was injured. 'Bapu wrote to Sardar Patel about the incident. He wrote to him, "It was Kalyanam who saved me from the mob attack." I considered it my duty to protect him.'

On the 4th of September, representatives of the local Hindu and Muslim communities met Bapu and gave him a written promise that read: Peace and quiet has been restored in Calcutta once again. We shall never again allow communal strife in the city, and we shall strive unto death to prevent it.

Bapu then agreed to call off his fast, but stayed back in Beliaghatta until the 9th of September.

On the 9th, he and his entourage started their journey to Delhi—his first trip to the city since it had become the capital of independent India. This journey too was no different. As they had done in the past, all of them travelled by third class in train.

Kalyanam remembers that at each railway station along the way, large numbers of people crowded the platform to meet Bapu. But he didn't talk to anyone; he just waved.

'The look on his face made it quite evident that he was very upset. He also decided to get off at the last stop before Delhi where Sardar Patel was to receive him, because he had been told that a large crowd awaited him in Delhi. But he didn't want to face the people of the country. He felt he had let them down by being unable to stop the division of the country.'

The rest of them, including Kalyanam, travelled up to Delhi with the luggage.

This time around, Bapu was not going to stay in the Bhangi Colony, as all of the available huts in every single open space in Delhi was taken up by Hindu and Sikh refugees fleeing the violence in what was now Pakistan. The refugees had lost everything, to their last penny.

Gandhiji was thus forced to stay at the palatial Birla House, a total contrast to the hut next to the sweepers in Bhangi Colony where he lived before he travelled to Calcutta.

There was a time when nobody said India could win her independence by non-violence. But now that independence has become a reality, we are bidding fair to say goodbye to non-violence. If India has no further use for Ahimsa, can she have any for me? I would not be in the least surprised if in spite of all the homage that the national leaders pay to me, they will one day say, 'We have had enough of this old man. Why does he not leave us alone?' No single person can eradicate misery or poverty during his lifetime. Unfortunately, however, what is equally true is that those delegated with powers to translate plans into action can add considerably to the misery of the people by their inaction. This is what exactly is happening in India today.

— Mahatma Gandhi

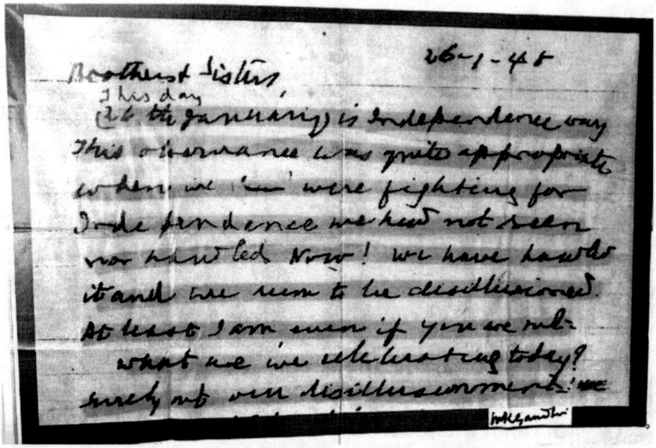

26-1-48

Brothers & Sisters,

This day (26th January) is Independence Day. This observance was quite appropriate when we were fighting for Independence we had not seen nor handled. Now! we have handled it and we seem to be disillusioned. At least I am even if you are not.

What are we celebrating today? Surely not our disillusionment! we

M.K.Gandhi

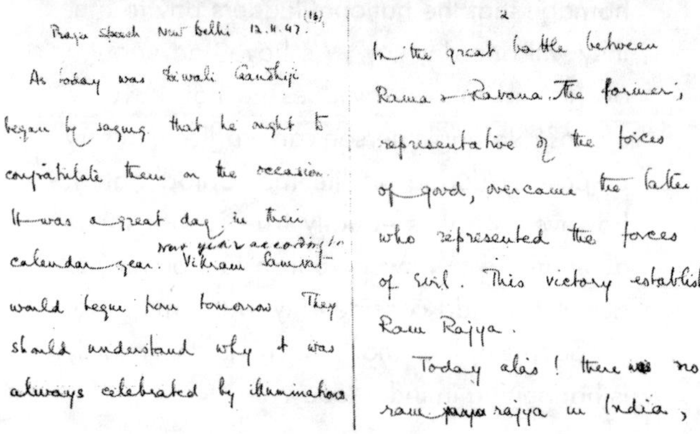

Prayer speech New Delhi 12.11.47. (18)

As today was Diwali Gandhiji began by saying that he ought to congratulate them on the occasion. It was a great day in their calendar year. Vikram Samvat new year according to would begin from tomorrow. They should understand why it was always celebrated by illuminations

2

In the great battle between Rama & Ravana, the former, representative of the forces of good, overcame the latter who represented the forces of evil. This victory established Ram Rajya.

Today alas! there is no ram rajya in India,

Message of the Mahatma on the 26th of January 1948 (Upper)

Prayer speech on November 1947 in Kalyanam's handwriting (Lower)

In Birla House

September 1947-January 1948

Owned by GD Birla, the Birla House on Albuquerque Road in New Delhi is where Gandhiji spent the last 144 days of his life; from the 9th of September 1947 to the 30th of January, 1948. It was here that he was assassinated by Nathuram Godse at a prayer meeting. Birla House is now a museum dedicated to Gandhiji's life and known as Gandhi Smriti. Government of India acquired the Old Birla House in 1971 and converted it into a National Memorial and it was opened to the public on 15th of August 1973. The museum has preserved Mahatma Gandhi's room and the prayer ground where he used to hold prayer meetings every evening. The building and the landscape remain as it was when the Mahatma lived.

On the very first day of his arrival in Delhi, Bapu visited the Jamia Millia Islamia to see Zakir Hussain and spent an hour talking to him about the situation in Delhi. He then visited some of the refugee camps. It was a sad and disturbed Gandhi that reached the Birla House; making his way through the throngs of refugees flooding Delhi after having left behind their ancestral homelands that they were now told belonged to another country. The new government under Nehru and Sardar Patel were utterly clueless as to how to take care of them.

Gandhiji's room in the Birla House was on the ground floor; large and carpeted with an attached toilet. As Bapu always sat on the floor, a cotton mattress and a pillow were kept in one corner of the room. There was a low desk placed in front of the mattress for him to write. At the other end were a table and a chair where all of the letters addressed to Bapu were kept. Kalyanam recalls that Bapu sometimes slept on the carpeted floor at night, along with the rest of his staff and visitors.

Apart from Kalyanam, the other people with Bapu at Birla House were his grand-nieces Manu and Abha, Bisen, and the brother-and-sister duo of Pyarelal Nayyar and Sushila Nayyar.

Despite all the disturbances, Bapu continued his daily routine. He got up early at 3.30 am, ran a morning prayer that his people attended, dictated letters to Kalyanam, and then met the people and official delegations. Some of the subjects Bapu spoke on after the prayer were, simple things like asking people not to pluck flowers from the Birla House garden, maintain cleanliness of the premises etc.

'He used to ask people to bring old newspapers to spread on the ground to sit for the prayers as it was winter and cold in Delhi. One day, during the prayers, he recited from the Quran and it angered a few people who were among the crowd. Later, they were identified as people belonging to the RSS and the Hindu Maha Sabha', Kalyanam recalls.

He also fondly remembers a goat they had kept in the Birla House garden as Bapu had only goat's milk. 'The goat had a good time there, with a clean yard to stay in and green grass to eat. Those who came to meet Bapu used to pat the goat, scratch her and even massage her. Some used to say, it was lucky to be of service to the Mahatma.'

Because they were guests at Birla House, those in charge of the house took care of all their needs. But as was the usual practice, his grand-daughters cooked Bapu's food, without salt. Though the British had left India, he continued the practise of not eating salt and sticking to select vegetables.

As Kalyanam's parents lived in Delhi, they made idlis and sent them for Bapu. Under Kalyanam's instructions, his mother prepared the idlis without salt. Bapu, a poor eater as always, ate only one idli.

Every morning, Birla used to visit the Mahatma when he dictated letters to Kalyanam just to enquire whether everything was all right. At first, Bapu had a plan to go back to Sevagram for ten days, from the 3rd of February 1948, as he felt his presence was not needed in Delhi. But when he found that the communal situation in Delhi was still not under control, Bapu wrote a letter in Hindi to Kishorelal Mashruwala of Sevagram, informing him that he was planning to be at Sevagram from the 3rd of February to the 12th but he was doubtful whether he would be able to make it. It turned out to be true. He couldn't go to Sevagram at all.

Birla was quite upset with his decision to go back to Sevagram. So, he told Bapu, 'Why do you want to go back to Sevagram? I am giving you this entire house. Just give me a big bathroom; I don't want anything else. You can have the entire Birla House to yourself.' Gandhiji just laughed at the suggestion and asked, 'Why do I need the entire Birla House?'

'Birla was a great philanthropist and he used to tell Bapu, "Whenever you want something, just tell me." He was the man who developed the ashram for Gandhiji, and he was one person who had absolute faith in Bapu's philosophy and was always there for Bapu. Bapu knew that he could rely on Birla. That was the kind of relationship they had.'

As days moved by, one day, Gandhiji told the girls who spent every single minute of their life serving him, 'You are looking after me all the time. You bring me food, give me massages, and give me baths. But you are not getting any exercise. You are young girls, you must do some exercise every day.' When they told him that they had no time to exercise, he asked them to go out for a walk for half-an-hour each morning. They then told him that they didn't know Delhi well enough to go out on walks.

Bapu then looked at Kalyanam and said, 'Kalyanam is from Delhi. Go with him.' So Kalyanam was assigned the task of taking the girls for a walk in the morning. Kalyanam was about twenty-four then and the girls, Manu and Abha were around twenty. From then on, the youngsters went out in the mornings for a walk.

One day, as they stepped out of the Birla House, they saw GD Birla coming out from the other door. He asked the girls where they were going so early in the morning. When they told him that Bapu had instructed them to go for morning walks with Kalyanam, he said, 'I go for my morning walks with [Sardar Vallabhbhai] Patel [independent India's first Home Minister and Deputy Prime Minister]. Why don't you join us?' He asked them to hop into the car. Kalyanam sat in the front and the girls and Birla sat at the back.

The car went straight to Patel's official residence and stopped in front of the gate for Patel, who was a favourite of Birla and also a friend, to join in the walk. The car was parked there and all of them crossed the road to Lodhi Gardens and walked there.

'Those were the days when there was no security around the Deputy Prime Minister's house. There was only one man guarding the gate. He did not stop and search visitors, or question them in any way. All of the refugees knew that they could meet Sardar Patel just as they did Gandhiji. At least ten or twenty people visited him regularly and they waited near the gate in the mornings so that they could meet him after his walk.'

An incident, which Kalyanam says he can never forget, happened one day after the walk. 'We saw Patel stopping to talk to some of the refugees who had gathered to air their grievances to him. They said, "Sir, we are living in the Paharganj locality and the Muslims in the area are creating a lot of trouble. They throw stones at us, and threaten to kill us." It was evident that the complainants were Hindus. Patel listened to their story patiently. He then asked, "How far is your place from here?" They said, "about six-seven miles." The next question was, "how have you come?" They told him that they took a bus and then walked, and it took them an hour to reach his house. His reaction was, "so, you wasted one hour and that too, spending some money, to tell me that you are troubled by the Muslims? Why don't you hit back?"'

Birla, who stood there listening to the conversation, kept quiet. But Manu Gandhi started giggling at Patel's remark.

Those days, before Bapu went to bed, it was gossip time with the three of them—Manu, Abha and Kalyanam sitting next to him. While Manu did all the gossiping, the other two just listened, smiling and laughing. 'That was the time we used to tell him all that was happening around. I never used to talk. Manu would tell him where we went for the walk, whom we met, the condition of the refugees etc etc. That particular evening, she told Bapu what Patel said in the morning, and giggled.'

'A surprised Bapu just asked, "Did he ask them to hit back? It's not a matter to giggle at." From that day onwards, he used to say, "Patel has changed and it was not the same Patel, whom I knew thirty years ago."'

He was a little worried that his own lieutenant, whom he had trained so far not to do any harm to others and not to treat Muslims in that manner, spoke so casually. Later on, whenever a Hindu-Muslim trouble arose, and differences between Patel and Nehru cropped up, Bapu gave the impression that he sided with Nehru. But he tried to patch up their strife so that the government ran smoothly. Both of them offered to resign twice and Bapu had to persuade them to continue.

During the day, a large chunk of Bapu's time was spent meeting the refugees from Pakistan at Birla House. He took upon himself the responsibility of wiping their tears away as best as he could. From morning, refugees stood in queue in front of Birla House to meet Gandhiji and tell him of their woes. It hurt him to hear the stories of neglect and corruption.

Other than the grieving refugees, one regular visitor to the Birla House was KC Niyogi, the Refugees and Rehabilitation Minister. It was his duty to take care of the millions of refugees by providing them with food, shelter, education and basic medical facilities. But there was an entire network of middlemen who made money. Help did not reach the needy and corruption was rampant. All of the refugees made a beeline to the Birla House to meet Gandhiji and air their complaints.

Kalyanam was in charge of letting people in to see Gandhiji. 'From the crowd, I would get about fifty people to stand apart before I took them in. I took them in to his room so that they could see and talk to him.'

This went on every day, from morning, through to the evening. Refugees complained to Bapu that they were not getting their due share because there were middlemen pocketing the money meant for them.

When he started receiving so many complaints of neglect, Bapu decided to go to the refugee camps to see the conditions. Kalyanam also accompanied him. 'We used to go almost everyday and would visit more than a dozen refugee camps. When we went, a large crowd of people, including journalists, came with us. When the refugees saw him, they would run to him with a litany of complaints. They also complained against the ministers who refused to listen to their woes. Bapu promised them that he would look into every compliant. At the same time, he also told them to be honest and serve others. But nobody did that! Everybody was self-obsessed.'

When they visited a particular refugee camp that was particularly dirty, Gandhiji asked them why this was the case. The refugees complained that that no sweepers had been assigned to the camp. This infuriated him! He told them that the government could only provide them with food, education, schools and dispensaries. But it was their duty to keep the area they lived in clean. He told them that there was nothing wrong in sweeping their own premises and it was not below their dignity to do so.

That was Bapu's advice for achieving a Swachch Bharat (Clean India)—advice that nobody took then, and nobody takes even today.

Many letters addressed to Mahatma Gandhi also reached Birla House and it was Kalyanam's responsibility to go through them and convey the message to Gandhi. When Kalyanam told him about the complaints, Bapu asked him to forward the letters to the respective ministries. 'There was a lot of corruption everywhere. Congressmen were living in splendour. Though Bapu urged them to lead a simple life, they lived in big bungalows and drove around in big cars. They had no time to meet the refugees or take care of their needs.'

It was not just the refugees, but ordinary people from all around the country, who also complained. Within weeks of independence, Gandhiji was flooded with complaints from all over India that charged the government with having let them down by not fulfilling the promises they had made during the freedom struggle. The complaints against the Congress leaders were those of corruption, nepotism, favouritism, black marketing, squandering public funds and leading lives of luxury.

Second October 1947 dawned. It was the Mahatma's 78th birthday. When birthday and congratulatory messages started pouring in from the morning, Bapu was in a bad mood; he who wanted to live till he was 125 was a disillusioned man. He said in his weak voice, 'Why do you people congratulate me? More appropriate would have been condolence messages. There is nothing but anguish in my mind. I have lost all desire to live, let alone for 125 years.'

He spoke about his anguish over what was happening in the country in his post-prayer speeches and wrote about it in his weekly newspaper Harijan. As Kalyanam was the one who either wrote or typed what he dictated, he remembered the range of topics on which Bapu offered advice. 'Until Gandhiji came into the picture, the Congress was an ordinary organisation. It was he who turned the Congress into the leaders of the independence movement. He was disheartened and disillusioned when partition took place. He was all the more disheartened to see the attitude of the newly-anointed ministers of independent India.

'He advised all of the ministers on good governance for the well-being of the people, but his advice was spurned by those to whom the destiny of the nation had been entrusted. He set out guidelines for the conduct of ministers, governors and ambassadors so that their lifestyle was in tune with the poverty and backwardness of the people. But none of them listened to him and they all lead a very ostentatious life.'

Bapu felt helpless at not being able to control those in power; he could only forward the complaints to the ministers and hope for the best. So frustrated and desperate was he that one day, he said, 'I do not wish to be a living witness to the many undesirable things that are going on in the country today. I am not responsible for what is going on. The government does not listen to me. I wish God takes me away. There was a time when whatever I said, the masses followed. Today mine is a voice in the wilderness. I am a back number. My teachings fall on stony ground. I am not the current coin I fancied I once was.'

During this time, another storm was brewing: the clashes between Jawaharlal Nehru, the Prime Minister, and Sardar Vallabhbhai Patel, the Deputy Prime Minister and Home Minister, began to aggravate. This worried Gandhiji intensely. It was a well-known fact that Gandhiji had a soft corner for Nehru as his family had donated a lot of money for the country. His father, Motilal Nehru gave his Anand Bhavan to the Congress and also did a lot for Gandhiji.

The incident that lit the powder keg was a dispute between the Hindus and the Muslims in Ajmer, Rajasthan. Somebody at the scene sent a telegram to Nehru. Instead of passing it on to Patel's Home Ministry, Nehru bypassed him entirely, and sent his private secretary over to look into the matter. Kalyanam was present when Patel complained to Gandhiji that Nehru was 'interfering' in his work.

This was followed by another incident when Sudhir Ghosh, a personal emissary of Bapu before independence, was appointed by the new government as the PRO under VK Krishna Menon at the Indian High Commission in London. While the High Commission was under Nehru's charge, the PRO came under the Information and Broadcasting Ministry, of which Sardar Patel was the minister.

'It was well known to everyone that Menon was an alter ego of Nehru and he suspected Sudhir Ghosh to be a Patel loyalist. So, there was a simmering discontent between Menon and Ghosh from day one, and one day, Menon suspended Ghosh from service and appointed another person in his place. Menon also manoeuvred to have external publicity taken over from the I&B Ministry by the Minister of External Affairs. Ghosh came back to Delhi and spoke to Bapu while Menon came and spoke to Nehru of the goings on. Anyway, Ghosh didn't go back to London, and was made a Member of the Rajya Sabha, clearly indicating who had the upper hand in the circumstances', Kalyanam recalls.

Another issue that brought forth the differences between the two most powerful members of then India's cabinet was the Princely State of Kashmir. While most of the princely states that were physically contiguous with India acceded to the Indian Union, the Hindu Maharaja of Kashmir, Hari Singh, was vacillating as he ruled over a Muslim-majority population. In 1948, as the Maharaja tried to make up his mind, Pakistan-supported tribesmen from the North-West Frontier Province invaded Kashmir. When they entered his territories, Hari Singh hurriedly signed the executed the Instrument of Accession and took the Princely State into the India Union.

Sardar Patel, the Home Minister, could convince 560 of the 562 Princely States that eventually acceded to join the Union without the use of force. He had to send the army in to capture the Muslim-ruled Hindu majority states of Hyderabad and Junagadh.

But this was not to be with Kashmir. The Indian troops pushed the tribesmen back, but were forced to stop when Nehru took the case to the United Nations; the territories not recovered by India are still under Pakistani rule (Pakistan occupied Kashmir). This became yet another bone of contention between the two men.

Then arose the promise India made to Pakistan to pay Rs 55 crore as part of the second instalment of arrears to be paid to it under the terms of the division of India's assets and liabilities following partition. Patel was totally against giving them the money as he believed Pakistan would use the money to buy arms and ammunition that they would use to attack Kashmir again. When Bapu came to know of the Indian government's non-payment, he spoke to Patel.

Kalyanam was witness to the argument they had. Patel tried to make him realise that the Pakistanis would use the money to commit aggression which, in a way, was true. When Patel refused to agree to pay the money, Bapu said that India had to honour a promise made. He did not stop arguing with Patel until an upset Patel told him, 'Bapu, you know nothing of administration.' Patel's argument was that while you could show your other cheek when slapped, in the administrative world, you would also ensure that the person who slapped you was booked for the offence. Patel walked out in a huff.

'Gandhiji decided to use his last weapon: to go on a fast, leaving Patel with no other option but pay Pakistan Rs 55 crore. It was not just Patel, everybody in the Indian government was very upset about the incident. The truth was, Bapu's way of dealing with things did not work when actually governing a country.'

That was his second fast after India became independent. Though he succeeded in achieving his goal in both the fasts, he had to pay the price with his life. 'In a way, this fast was a cause for his death, as it angered many in India because he forced the Indian government to pay Rs 55 crore to Pakistan', Kalyanam says frankly.

Difference between the party and the government was also brewing by then. On the 15th of November 1947, Acharya Kripalani [the president of the Congress Party during the transfer of power from Britain to India] resigned from the post of the AICC president, saying he had not been consulted nor taken into confidence by the government where Congressmen fought amongst themselves. Kripalani said, 'it is the party from which the government derives its power but the government ignores the party.'

Kripalani asked Bapu sarcastically, 'Bapu, you always ask people to love their enemies. Why don't you ask them to love their friends first?' Bapu supported Kripalani's stand on the matter.

'Popularity of Nehru and Patel enabled them to dominate the party. They identified themselves as the party. They did not like the Congress president curbing their power, and they did not want to give him a veto in their proposals. They wanted to elect a new party president who would be a puppet, who would obey the government', Kalyanam observes.

At the next Congress Working Committee meeting, Gandhiji was also present to elect a new party president. As it was his day of silence, he wrote the name of Narendra Dev, a socialist leader, on a piece of paper and passed it on to Nehru. Though Nehru supported his candidature, the others opposed it.

'The morning session ended at 10 am without taking a vote on the issue. At noon, Nehru and Patel, without consulting Bapu, urged Rajendra Prasad to be a candidate. At 1 pm, he came to Birla House and informed Bapu about his candidature but Bapu did not agree with the idea. Rajendra Prasad promised to withdraw his candidacy but subsequently, he was persuaded by Nehru and Patel not to do so, and he became the new president of the Congress party. Bapu sent a note to me on this development. That was how Rajendra Prasad became the party president after Acharya Kripalani.'

As time went on, Bapu realised that the India that had risen out of the ashes of British imperialism was not the free India of his dreams...

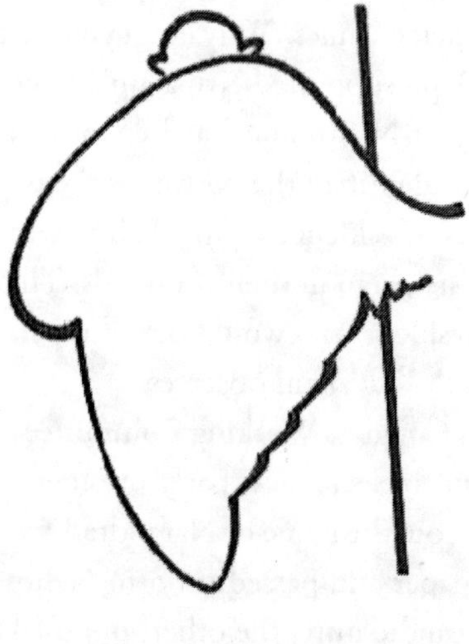

My religion teaches me that, whenever there is distress which one cannot remove, one must fast and pray. The fasts are a part of my being. I can as well do without my eyes, for instance, as I can without fasts. What the eyes are for the outer world, fasts are for the inner. I do not undertake them for my amusement. I would not torture the flesh for the love of fame. Though I bear joyfully the pangs of hunger and many other discomforts of fasting, let no one imagine that I do not suffer. These fasts are bearable only because they are imposed upon me by a higher Power and the capacity to bear the pain also comes from that Power. I cannot fast at the dictation of anyone. Such fasts [unto death] cannot be lightly undertaken. They can conceivably be wholly undesirable. They cannot be undertaken out of anger. Anger is a short madness. I must, therefore, undertake the fast only when the still small voice within me calls for it. A genuine fast cleanses the body, mind and soul. It crucifies the flesh and to that extent sets the soul free. A sincere prayer can work wonders. It is an intense longing of the soul for its even greater purity. Purity thus gained, when it is utilised for a noble purpose, becomes a prayer. I believe that there is no prayer without fasting, and there is no real fast without prayer. A complete fast is a complete and literal denial of the self. It is the truest prayer. 'Take my life and let it be, always, only, all for Thee' is not, should not be, a mere lip or figurative expression. It has to be reckless and joyous giving without the least reservation. Abstention from food and even water is but the mere beginning, the least part of the surrender. The weapon of fasting, I know, cannot be lightly wielded. It can easily savour of violence unless it is used by one skilled in the art. I claim to be such an artist in this subject.

—Mahatma Gandhi

The End
30 January 1948

> Even if I am to be murdered, I will bear no ill will towards anyone. I would rather pray to God to grant better sense to the person(s) who murder me.
>
> —Mahatma Gandhi

Every single day that followed the 15th of August 1947 was disturbing and painful for the man who spent his life striving to see an independent India. The man who'd once expressed a desire to go on living wished his life would end quickly after India attained its independence in the shadow of bloodshed and violence. He said, 'I have no desire to live long. Terrible things are happening all around.'

Because of his stance on Pakistan, like demanding that the Indian government pay the Pakistani government its dues, he had many enemies within India by then. From a national hero who united the masses, he'd gone on to become the target of verbal and physical attacks by sections of the public for this and for the misdeeds of Congressmen in power at the Centre and the States. People looked up to Gandhiji as the man who'd won them freedom. Naturally, when independent India's government failed to take care of them, they—especially the refugees fleeing the violence in Pakistan—looked at it as his failure.

In spite of feeling helpless in the face of misgovernance at home and acrimony with a neighbour that was a part of home just a few months earlier, Gandhiji went ahead as usual with his routine of prayer meetings, dictations to his secretaries and meetings with the public on the grounds of Birla House.

The 20th of January 1948 was a first indication of what was to come just ten days later. A Punjabi refugee, who'd fled what was now Pakistan, tossed a bomb at him as his prayer meeting was in progress.

'There were only 200-300 people that day at the prayer meeting. A bomb fell on the boundary wall of the compound, just fifteen yards away from the rostrum, and exploded with a loud thud. I was sitting next to Bapu, and I thought the military was practising rifle shooting. I am sure Bapu heard the noise too, but he didn't pay much attention to it', Kalyanam says as he recalls what happened that day.

After the prayer meeting had come to an end, they came to know that the noise was not the military practising rifle shooting. In fact, the gardener caught hold of the person who'd tossed the bomb as he tried to escape and handed him over to the police. He was a Hindu refugee from the Montgomery district in west

Punjab and had lost his parents during the partition. He held the Mahatma responsible for their killing. He confessed while questioning that he had indeed thrown the bomb as he did not like Bapu's peace campaign. He had come to Delhi from Bombay a week earlier and was living in a mosque in Paharganj. When he was asked to go away from the mosque by the police, it angered him immensely.

The government was naturally worried about what happened. Gandhiji's safety was their first priority, they said. In the early hours of the morning of the 21st, Sardar Vallabhbhai Patel, the Home Minister and the Deputy Prime Minister, issued orders to the police that the pockets of every person entering the Birla House to see Gandhi or participate in the prayer meetings in the evenings be searched.

By 11am, a sub-inspector from the nearby police station came to see Kalyanam. He told Kalyanam of the search orders he'd received from higher up. 'At that point, I was responsible for Gandhiji's affairs—people had to take my permission before they got to meet Bapu or to post somebody as a guard for him. After having heard the sub-inspector out and knowing Bapu, I told him that he could have guards but couldn't search everybody's pockets, as that would be insulting to visitors. But he insisted that they had to search everyone as somebody might try and smuggle a dagger, a gun or a bomb in to try and kill Bapu. After the incident of the previous day, I realised the danger Bapu's life was in. As a result, I decided to speak to Bapu and take his permission before I gave the police the go-ahead.'

As expected, Gandhiji refused to allow the police to institute the searches they wished to. The policeman reported Gandhiji's refusal on to the higher authorities. The Deputy Inspector General (DIG) of the Delhi Police then decided to visit Kalyanam.

The DIG told Kalyanam, 'It is the duty of the police to see that Gandhiji comes to no harm. If his life is lost, the police will be blamed by the people for not having protected him. So, I would like to speak to Gandhiji.'

Kalyanam took him to Gandhiji. 'Bapu looked up at the police officer and asked, "What are you going to do?" He replied that the police would search the pockets of all those who came to the prayer meeting. Bapu shot down the request, saying, he would not allow that. He said, "When you go to a temple to pray, is it right to search your pockets? If you want to search the pockets of those who come for my prayer meetings, I'll just stop running them." The police officer then politely said, "Sir, we will be blamed if somebody tried to kill you and we were unable to stop him."'

But Bapu could be a very obstinate man. 'He said, "nobody can kill me, only God can kill me. I am in God's hands. Even if you assign 10,000 policemen to protect me, you will not be able to save my life if God decides to take it away. Those who prefer security to freedom have no right to live."'

The DIG had to give in, in the face of Bapu's dogged refusals. He assured Bapu that no searches would be instituted before leaving.

Following his refusal, the police had no option but post plainclothes men to stand outside and keep a watch on suspicious people who might potentially try to attack Gandhiji on his way to the prayer meetings and back. The earlier guard of four policemen outside Birla House was reinforced by sixteen more armed policemen from that day.

Soon after the incident, some people who came to seek Bapu's darshan told Kalyanam that there was a conspiracy to kill Bapu. 'They told me that these people were operating from the Hindu Maha Sabha building in Reading Road, Delhi. I didn't take any serious note of this. In retrospect, I feel that had I conveyed this information to the police, the tragedy could have been avoided. I did not consider it necessary then because I hardly imagined that any person doing good to society would have any enemies at all.'

The 30th of January 1948, a Friday, dawned like any other day. Nobody but one man had the slightest inkling as to what was going to happen that evening. Not one person expected the day to be any different from the day before. Nobody thought of how their lives, and the destiny of a nation, were going to change very soon.

Everybody got up as usual at 3.30 in the morning. 'Bapu woke Abha up before going to the toilet. He came back from the toilet and sat on the mattress for his morning prayers. We also sat before him', Kalyanam remembers.

As usual, the morning prayers commenced with recitations from the scriptures of all religions, particularly Hinduism and Islam, in order to stress the unity of all religions. While they recited, Bapu closed his eyes in meditation as was his wont.

Abha was still asleep and was not part of the morning prayers, and he noticed her absence like he noticed the absence of any of the other members.

'Immediately after the prayer, Manu went to the kitchen to fetch Bapu's morning drink, a glass of hot water mixed with a tablespoonful of honey and lime. When she handed the marble tumbler to him, I heard him telling her in Gujarati, "It appears my influence, even among my close companions, is waning. Prayer is like a broomstick meant to cleanse one's soul. Abha's failure to participate in the prayer pains me. You are aware of the importance I attach to prayers. You may, on my behalf, convey my displeasure to her. If she is not willing to participate in the prayer, she should take leave of me. This will be in our joint interest!"'

By this time, Abha had woken up but Bapu did not ask her any questions. Direct confrontations were not Bapu's way of dealing with unpleasant issues. 'I continued to sit by his side to receive my instructions for the day. He wanted me to make arrangements for his visit to Sevagram for ten days, on the 2nd of February. He was still thinking of going back to Sevagram. I then placed before him the typed draft of the new constitution for the Indian National Congress that he had dictated to me the previous day. In this, he'd suggested its disbandment and reconstitution as a new body with greater emphasis on social service and rural uplift. He did not want to go through it. He called Pyarelalji [his other senior secretary] and handed the draft to him with instructions to peruse it carefully and make any suggestions or corrections that he may consider necessary', Kalyanam remembers the day quite vividly.

At two in the afternoon, after having taken Gandhiji's permission, Abha and Manu went to visit some of their friends, promising to return in time for the prayer meeting in the evening. So, the responsibility of serving Gandhiji's evening meal fell on Kalyanam.

'Although the government had been in office for only five months, the media was full of the alleged differences between Nehru and Patel. Gandhiji was distressed by these rumours and wanted to counter this. He was even thinking of asking Patel to resign, so that Nehru might have a free hand to conduct the affairs of the country. He summoned Patel for a discussion on the subject at 4 pm. Accompanied by his daughter Maniban, Patel arrived just as Gandhiji was having his early supper, so he wasn't able to speak with Bapu until a little later.'

The evening prayer meeting was to start at 5 pm but the discussions between Bapu and Patel continued beyond five. Everybody started getting worried. 'We knew what they were talking about, and how important and serious the matter was; naturally none of us dared to disturb them. Manu, who'd returned a little earlier, went in when it was 5:10 and told Bapu that the time for prayer had passed.

'I heard him admonishing the girl for not telling him earlier that he was running late for the prayer meeting. He told her that they were his time-keepers. "I am late. I do not like this at all." When Manu replied that they did not want to interrupt because of the serious nature of their talks, Gandhiji shot back, "It is the duty of a nurse to give medicines at the right time to the patient. If there is a delay, the patient may die."

'He then went to the toilet and walked straight to the prayer ground, which was nearly thirty-forty yards away. There were four or five steps to be climbed and then there was a big lawn. He knew he was late by fifteen minutes for the prayer meeting and that showed in the way he walked. There were about 250 people anxiously awaiting his arrival. I could see from the distance that everybody there was looking at Bapu's room. As he came out, someone noticed him and shouted, "Here comes Gandhiji."

'Soon, every single person was looking in his direction. Bapu walked briskly as usual, with his head bent and his glance glued to the ground, supporting himself on the shoulders of Manu and Abha. I followed closely to his left.

'We ascended the steps leading to the prayer platform. People stood with folded hands and Bapu reciprocated with folded hands. When people touched his feet and said, "pranam", he blessed them. Then, one person bowed down, as if he was kneeling to touch his feet. There was nothing unusual about what he did. He got up, and shot Bapu. He fired three consecutive shots. I missed a bullet by a few inches. What happened after that is hazy. Bapu fell down, bleeding profusely. In the melee, his spectacles and slippers fell away. I was too shocked and dumb-founded to react. People around me were shouting and crying loudly.'

The news spread fast. Within minutes, there was a huge crowd outside Birla House and they had to close the gate to prevent people from entering the premises. Soon, somebody carried Bapu's body to his room, but the wailing crowd also scrambled to collect something belonging to him as a souvenir.

'They even scooped handful of earth from the place where Bapu fell to the assassin's bullet, leaving a big pit there within hours. We cordoned off the area and posted a guard outside the gate.'

Kalyanam rushed to his room and called Nehru's office and told them the news. 'After having informed the Prime Minister's office, I pushed my way through the crowd, got into a car and rushed to [Sardar Vallabhbhai] Patel's house to inform him of the calamity. He'd left Birla House just before the prayer meeting had started. It was to him that Bapu spoke last.'

Sardar Patel was too shocked to react when Kalyanam broke the news to him. After all, he had spoken to him just a few minutes ago.

Later Patel said, 'I had personally pleaded with Bapu to permit the police to do their duty in regard to his protection but without success. To my profound regret and utter sorrow and to the irreparable loss for all of us, the nation and the world, the weak spot both I and the police had spotted was deceitfully and successfully exploited by the assassin, and Gandhiji's prophetic words have come true; that, if he had to die, nobody could save him.'

After informing all the important people in the government, Kalyanam was back at Birla House to sit near Bapu's body. 'There he lay on the mat with people around him. He looked as if he was asleep. I touched him and found that his body was still warm. Nobody could forget that night. It was a terrible day for not just us but for the millions of people all over the world for whom he lived and died. It was only later, as I sat alone, that tears came to my eyes. Till then, I was in such a state of shock that not a single tear came out of my eyes. The gravity of the situation, the bitter truth… all dawned on me as I sat next to him. I thought, a great man had been killed: a man who believed in non-violence, a man who wouldn't harm a living thing. It was such a man that had been put to death by a violent man. He didn't deserve such a death….'

Not a single person in Delhi slept the entire night; thousands of people walked past the body and there was not a single soul without tears in their eyes. 'In his last few post-prayer speeches, Bapu had been repeatedly expressing the wish that God take him away since he did not want to be a silent witness to the monstrous barbarities that were going on in the country. I thought that maybe, God had answered his prayer through the assassin.'

Kalyanam, however, does not remember hearing Bapu say 'Hey Ram' after he was shot. 'People say that Bapu said, "Hey

Ram." But I don't know if he did. There was chaos after the shots were fired. Perhaps he said it, perhaps he didn't. But I didn't hear anything; I was maybe too shocked at that moment. But people have said that they heard him say, Hey Ram! If you heard it, it is alright but as far as I'm concerned, I didn't.'

The cremation at Rajghat was arranged for the 31st of January. There remained the question of who would light his funeral pyre.

Bapu had four sons, and he had disowned his eldest son, Harilal Gandhi, for his drinking and smoking habits. In any case, he was in Bombay on the day of Gandhiji's death and didn't come for the cremation. Instead, he sent a telegram. His second son, Manilal Gandhi, ran an ashram in South Africa and couldn't make it to India at such short notice. So it was his third son Ramdas Gandhi, a superintendent at Tata Oil Mills in Nagpur, who performed his last rites. His youngest son Devdas Gandhi was also present.

By four in the evening on the 31st of January1948, Bapu's body was carried to Rajghat and cremated there amidst loud cries and chanting of *Ram Naam Satya hai*. It was as if entire India was at Rajghat to bid him good-bye.

That was the end of Kalyanam's very close association of four years with the Mahatma. 'I consider him a unique personality. He believed in non-violence and never harmed anybody with his words or deeds. He never spoke ill of anybody. He always spoke the truth and always wanted to do the right thing. He wanted people to live in peace and disliked war. He led a very simple life. It may take another 2000 years for the world to see another person like Bapu. He lived his entire life for the country but died a disillusioned, disheartened, disenchanted and disappointed man.'

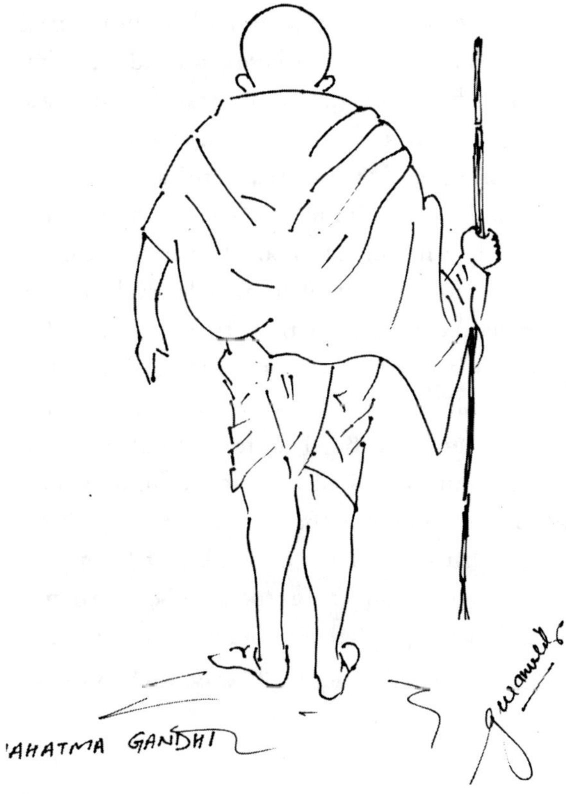

I think that the word 'saint' should be ruled out of present life. It is too sacred a word to be lightly applied to anybody, much less to one like myself who claims only to be a humble searcher after Truth, knows his limitations, makes mistakes, never hesitates to admit them when he makes them, and frankly confesses that he, like a scientist, is making experiments about some 'of the eternal verities' of life, but cannot even claim to be a scientist because he can show no tangible proof of scientific accuracy in his methods or such tangible results of his experiments as modern science demands. To clothe me with sainthood is too early even if it is possible. I myself do not feel a saint in any shape or form. But I do feel I am a votary of Truth in spite of all my errors of unconscious omission and commission. I remain an optimist, not that there is any evidence that I can give that right is going to prosper, but because of my unflinching faith that right must prosper in the end.... Our inspiration can come only from our faith that right must ultimately prevail. Those who have at all followed my humble career even superficially cannot have failed to observe that not a single act of my life has been done to the injury of any individual or nation... I claim no infallibility. I am conscious of having made Himalayan blunders, but I am not conscious of having made them intentionally or having even harboured enmity towards any person or nation, or any life, human or sub-human. I cannot intentionally hurt anything that lives, much less fellow-human beings, even though they may do the greatest wrong to me and mine.

It would be impossible for any person to point to a single act of mine during the past fifty years which could be proved to have been antagonistic to any person or community. I have never believed anyone to be my enemy. My faith demands that I should consider no one as such. I may not wish ill to anything that lives.

— Mahatma Gandhi

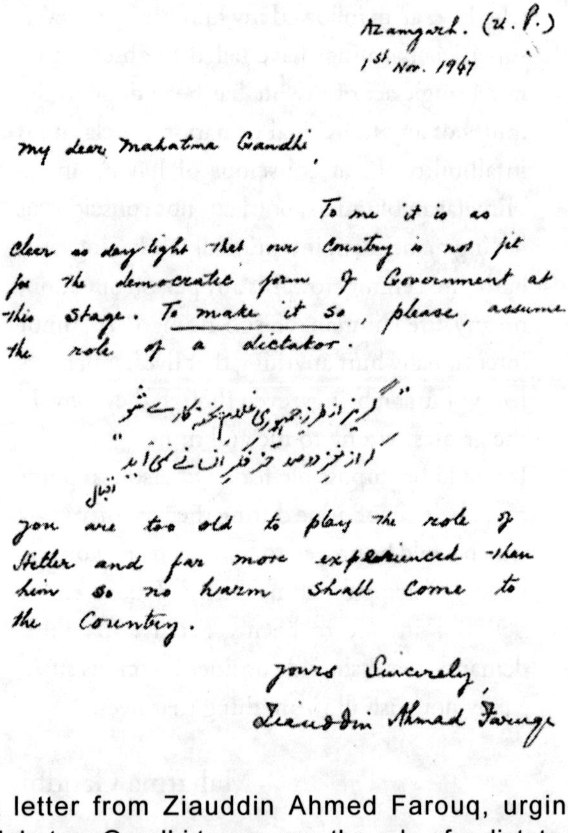

Azamgarh. (U.P.)
1st Nov. 1947

My dear Mahatma Gandhi,

To me it is as clear as day light that our Country is not fit for the democratic form of Government at this stage. To make it so, please, assume the role of a dictator.

[illegible]
[illegible]
اقبال

You are too old to play the role of Hitler and far more experienced than him so no harm shall come to the Country.

Yours Sincerely,
Ziauddin Ahmad Faruqi

A letter from Ziauddin Ahmed Farouq, urging Mahatma Gandhi to assume the role of a dictator

His Days After Bapu

One of the things Kalyanam did on the 31st of January 1948 was to send a man to Palai Bank in Connaught Circus to take back from the bank a cheque he'd deposited two days earlier.

'I always used to carry some money with me, Rs 30-40, whenever I travelled, even though I never had any need for it when travelling with Bapu. I never took any money from Bapu for working with him; as far as I was concerned, it was a godsend opportunity to serve a man as great as him.

'One day, when we were in Calcutta, a woman who had come to visit Bapu needed some money. As usual, he didn't have any money on him. He turned to me and asked, "Kalyanam, do you have any money on you?" I had Rs 35 on me, which I immediately handed over. He passed it on to the woman. Though Bapu asked me to collect the money from him later, I forgot about it completely, for I did not see it as a loan.'

But Bapu didn't forget the incident. A few days later, Bapu gave Kalyanam a signed cheque for Rs 35. Kalyanam kept the cheque on his person until they were back in Delhi. On the 29th of January 1948, he deposited the cheque in the bank. And as we all know, Bapu departed this Earth on the next day.

'I wanted to get the cheque back from the bank before it cleared. Bapu always used to talk about living until he was 125, I never expected to see him die before me. As a result, the thought never came to my mind that I might want to preserve the letters he'd written or corrected. I handed to another associate the copies of everything I'd typed for him. The original manuscripts, however, weren't usually filed and stayed with me.

'I was perhaps ignorant at that time; I didn't think they were particularly valuable. I either threw them in the bin basket or gave them away to souvenir hunters. I must have given away at least 1,000 such letters of the Mahatma to various people. He never instructed me to preserve them, maybe because he also didn't attach any importance to them.'

But not only ordinary Indian citizens, even Lord Mountbatten used to collect the Mahatma's handwritten notes, Kalyanam remembers.

Kalyanam recalls an incident that reinforced his belief that Bapu didn't want the drafts to be preserved. 'We were staying at Birla House then. One day, while returning from an interview with the Viceroy, he had to urgently go to the toilet. He got out of the car and went to the toilet in my room. While coming out of the room, he saw piles of papers kept under my table. He first thought those were letters to be typed. When I explained that the typed versions were preserved and those were the drafts written by him, he said, "*Agar type kar liya hai to inko yahan kyon rakha hai? Phek do aur kamra saaf rakho [if you've already typed them, why do you need to keep them here? Throw them away and clean your room].*"' But Kalyanam couldn't get himself to throw them all way.

On the 13th day following his cremation, the Mahatma's ashes were taken for immersion at the Prayag in Allahabad. 'Two to three million men, women and children were present at the Prayag to witness the immersion. So many people had travelled from various parts of India by bus, train and plane to be in Allahabad at the time of immersion. Some of them had come by foot!'

'As the train came to a halt at the station, there was the sort of silence where one could hear a pin drop. Sarojini Naidu received the urn from the compartment and was at the head of the procession leading the way. Saffron-coloured planes showered flowers and rose petals from above. The urn passed a route of seven miles and finally his ashes became a part of the Ganga.'

And now, after spending four years of day and night in the company of the Mahatma, it was time for Kalyanam to move on. Soon, all of those who'd worked with the Mahatma had left Birla House.

To start with, the now-unemployed Kalyanam stayed at the house of Sardar Vallabhbhai Patel, the Deputy Prime Minister for a couple of days, and in those few days also, he helped the government monitor and assess the arrangements for the refugees. Because of his proximity to many leading politicians, many foreign newspapers wanted him to work for them in order to get 'inside news'. But Kalyanam refused all of them.

Around this time, Jawaharlal Nehru, India's first Prime Minister, asked Kalyanam to come work for him in the Prime

Minister's Office. He was given a room in Teen Murti Bhavan, Nehru's residence.

'For an hour each morning, Nehru would meet people who'd come from all parts of the land to submit petitions in the lawns of Teen Murti Bhavan. My job was to walk behind him and collect the petitions. It was not an exciting job by any means, but I had no problem doing so.'

But Kalyanam worked for Nehru for just a fortnight, and it wasn't the job that led him to leave.

'I left because I could not abide MO Mathai's behaviour. Mathai (the PM's assistant) lived in Teen Murti Bhavan too. Nehru would leave the building at about 9 pm each night to meet with foreign ambassadors and the like. Mathai would lie in wait in his room until Nehru had left. He would then head to the YWCA [Young Women's Christian Association] club and bring girls over from there to his room, where they would have a merry time drinking until Nehru got back. After having spent so many years with Bapu, I could not tolerate this. Only the peons and I were aware of this debauchery. I brought it to Nehru's attention, but he took no action. So, I decided to leave.'

But the incident did not ruin his relationship with Nehru; they stayed in touch until the latter's death. 'In fact, when he came to Madras a few years later, he came to my house. In those days, a Prime Minister could make such visits. His car was parked in front of my house and he came in like any other guest would. I wanted to serve him something and made a quick upma, of which he ate a little.'

After leaving his employment with the Prime Minister, Lady Mountbatten, the wife of the Governor General of India, asked him to help her. She was on a mission to rescue women and children who were abducted during the partition as the Chairperson of the United Council for Relief and Welfare. 'She knew me very well from my time with Bapu, and asked me whether I could help her with her work. I agreed. I always admired the way she conducted herself.'

Though she offered him a salary of a thousand rupees, he refused any money as he had decided never to accept a paisa as salary from the day he'd started working for Bapu. Moreover, she offered him food and a place to stay, which was nothing but the Viceregal Lodge [now Rashtrapathi Bhavan] where she also stayed. He agreed to work for her. 'I travelled with her and her staff in her personal Dakota plane. Everybody describes her as a beautiful lady. But she was quite old by the time I first met her, and looked it. But she was very kind and unassuming. I remember her coming to my room with her six puppies and saying, "Mr Kalyanam, breakfast is ready." Imagine a person of her stature coming to my room and calling me for breakfast! They [the British] were all such wonderful people and I miss them.'

His work with Lady Mountbatten continued until she left India for England in June 1948.

At this point, he joined Mirabehn in her ashram in Rishikesh. 'I stayed with her in her hut. She was the advisor to the UP government on agriculture. My job was to take dictations from her, type those letters and post them; quite similar to the work I did for Bapu. I was with her for about six months, until she too decided to go back to Europe.'

Following his stint with Mirabehn, he was sent by the Indian Government to China as a secretary to the Indian Goodwill

Mission. He had this opportunity because of how well-known he was to all the powers that be, from the Prime Minister downwards.

On his return from China, he got a Fellowship from the United Nations to study child welfare in Norway, Sweden, Finland and Israel. He spent the next eight months travelling in these countries.

In 1956, he was appointed as the Regional Commissioner for the Scheduled Castes and Scheduled Tribes. For the first time in his life, he moved to Madras, a place he hasn't left since. Though the entire south of India was under his domain, he stayed put in Madras.

It was in Madras in 1959 that, at the age of 38, he met his future wife, Saraswathi, in an office. They then proceeded to have two daughters, born in 1963 and 1965.

While working as the Commissioner for the Scheduled Castes and Scheduled Tribes, he heard that GD Birla had come to Madras. Having met Birla many times when he was with Bapu, and having stayed at Birla House for quite sometime, he had this desire to meet him. Though he got an appointment, Birla didn't recognise him at first.

'When I told him who I was, he immediately recognised me and was very happy to meet me after a decade. He was curious to know what I was doing and how I was doing. When I told him that I was living in a rented house but couldn't afford to buy my own house, he immediately gave me Rs 25,000 so that I could buy a house. He was always a generous person. He knew I'd never accepted any salary from Bapu. With that money, I bought the house I live in today; it is now worth crores!'

After working as the Commissioner for four-and-a-half years, Kalyanam had to leave the government job. The reason was—he had joined C Rajagopalachari's Swatantra Party. 'As a government servant, I was not supposed to join a political party. When I joined Rajaji's Swatantra Party, somebody complained against me and I had to resign from my job. Rajaji started the party because he was disillusioned with the Congress Party and felt it was not taking the nation in the right direction. I agreed with Rajaji. That's why I joined him.'

When Rajaji heard of Kalyanam's dismissal, he shot off a letter to Nehru complaining of the unfairness of it all. But Nehru replied to say that there was little he could do to interfere in matters such as these. As a result, Kalyanam ended up working for Rajaji and the Swatantra Party until Rajaji's demise.

'I used to go to Rajaji's office every morning to help him write letters, draft articles against the policies of the Central government and send press releases out to newspapers. Once again, I never accepted a salary. My admiration for Rajaji is boundless, and second only to my admiration for Bapu himself. His razor-sharp intellect was such that it drew Bapu's admiration. My experience of working for Rajaji was quite similar to working with Bapu. They were both simple, honest and intelligent people.'

Rajaji always appreciated Kalyanam's dedication and hard work and when he contributed a large sum of money to the Swatantra Party, he wrote Kalyanam a letter wherein he described him as a 'remarkable man'.

He was also among the guests at Kalyanam's wedding. Kalyanam remembers Rajaji coming over to his house for lunch one day. 'Though he was such an important man, he had no qualms coming to my house at my invitation. That's why I said he was like Bapu. I haven't seen a man like him since; they were such unique and rare personalities. Had Rajaji been younger when he'd broken away from the Congress Party, he probably would have succeeded in making it an alternative to the Congress.'

Another person he admired a lot was Khan Abdul Ghaffar Khan, with whom he had spent many days of his life. The love they shared was so deep that Ghaffar Khan visited him at his residence when he visited Madras in 1969, when India was celebrating the 100th birth anniversary of Mahatma Gandhi.

'I still remember how people were surprised to see him coming out of the flight, carrying a small bundle that had his clothes, brush etc under his arms. He always travelled like that but those who had invited him were not used to seeing such simple people. They asked him, "Sir, your suitcase?" He replied with a smile, "I don't have a suitcase. I have only this small bundle. I always travel with this bundle." That was Abdul Ghaffar Khan, simple and humble, like Bapu.'

When Kalyanam came to know that he was staying at Raj Bhavan, he sought an appointment with him. When they met, the first thing Kalyanam did was, fall at his feet. 'He was very happy to see me after so many years. We had spent so much time together at Sevagram and Bhangi Colony, and he was delighted to see me. I insisted that he visited my place and he did. When at my place, we reminisced about the old days. Both of us agreed that nobody seemed to follow Bapu's footsteps anymore. He was also extremely unhappy with the stand the Congress Party had taken and scathing in his criticism of Indira Gandhi's regime.

'When I told him how Rajaji had set up the Swatantra Party against Nehru, he remained silent; he was probably dismayed as he knew both of them very well.

'While I still remember that he didn't eat anything, he was there for a good half-an-hour, a half-hour I still cherish. I made sure to take photos of him with my young daughters before he left.'

Upon Rajaji's death in 1972, Kalyanam retired to a quiet life of cleaning and service to the community.

MARCH

OF TIME & PEOPLES

The People Say:

CONGRESS WORSE THAN THE BRITISH

★

'They are even cursing the Congress says veteran Congressman.

The front page of a newspaper dated 21 April 1948

Just 4 days before his assassination, on his day of silence (Monday) on 26th January 1948, after seeing the unnecessary and ostentatious Government celebrations on that Independence Day, Gandhi, overcomes by great anguish and inner sorrow, had recorded as follows:

26-01-1948

"Brothers & Sisters,
This day
(26th January) is Independence Day.
This observance was quite appropriate
When we were fighting for
Independence we had not seen
Nor handled. Now! We have handled
It and we seem to be disillusioned.
At least I am, even if you are not.
What are we celebrating today?
Surely not our disillusionment!"
M.K.Gandhi

I am presenting below the facsimile of the concerned extract from the original message of Gandhi dated 26-1-1948.

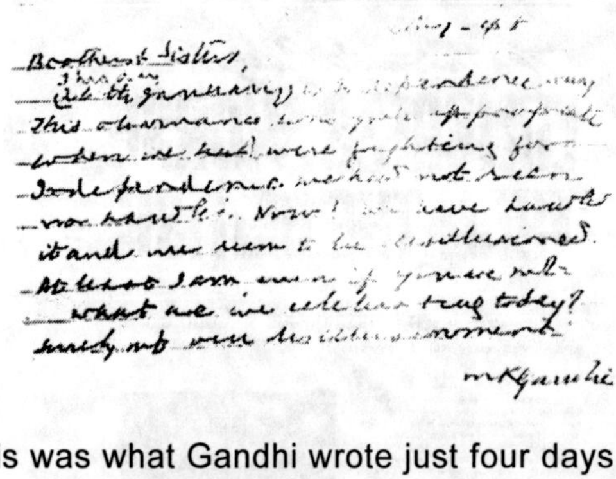

This was what Gandhi wrote just four days before his death. It was a Monday when he observed silence

Kalyanam's Thoughts

Kalyanam is one of the few people alive to have worked with both Sardar Vallabhbhai Patel and Nehru. When the debate rages today over the legacies of these two giants that bestrode the stage at the dawn of our nation, who better to join the debate than Kalyanam?

How relevant is Mahatma Gandhi and his philosophy today? This question is asked almost everyday, and not by Indians alone. What does the man who spent four years working closely with the man himself think? Even today, people have questions and suspicions about Mahatma Gandhi's sexual experiments, his lying naked with girls by his side. Did Kalyanam bear witness to these, and how did he react to them?

As I have had occasion to mention earlier in this very book, I have always been amazed by Kalyanam's obsession with cleanliness. Even at a frail ninety-three, whenever I went to his house, I always found him in the garden or on the terrace, cleaning up and tending to his plants. In 2015, cleanliness is back in the news with Narendra Modi's Swachch Bharat campaign. What does Kalyanam, the self-described 'sweeper par excellence', think of the initiative?

This chapter is written in the first person, and are on the basis of what Kalyanam told me during my long conversations with him:

Bapu and Today's India

When Indians have forgotten Gandhiji completely, he is more relevant today than any other time in the history of India and the world. The whole world is in turmoil. There is no peace anywhere. There will be peace on earth only if we were to live as Gandhiji implored us to. That is why I feel the world badly needs a person like him now.

While leaders like Obama are praising Gandhiji to the skies, India has forgotten him. If Gandhiji is forgotten today, it is because of the Congress. I am not for dynastic rule and I do not agree with the present-day Congress projecting the Nehru family as the only family that sacrificed for the cause of freedom. This new generation of Indians know nothing about Patel, Rajaji, Subhash Chandra Bose and the countless others who fought just as hard. It is unfair.

The truth is, Gandhiji was forgotten in 1947 itself, soon after independence. The new leaders were more interested in enjoying power than serving people. He trusted everybody, and that was the mistake he made. They were all his lieutenants and good people to start with, but they began to enjoy the luxuries that came with power, and grew more interested in making money than serving people. Why did Bapu lead such a simple life? Because he saw that the common man suffered; he couldn't afford the basic things in life. But none of our Parliamentarians emulate his example today. They want big bungalows, luxury cars and lots of servants. They should live like the poorest of the poor if they want to serve the people.

Bapu identified himself with the ordinary people of India. He wanted to be like them in order to seek their cooperation and help in throwing out the British rule. He gave up clothing in 1921 and walked around in a loincloth, he ate simple food, and he lived in a mud hut with no electricity, toilet and water facilities just as an ordinary villager might. He sacrificed everything and owned nothing, except a pair of spectacles, a pair of slippers, a pair of half dhotis, a copy each of the Quran, Bhagavad Gita and the Bible and an image of three monkeys (depicting speak no evil, hear no evil and see no evil) representing the philosophy he believed in.

After independence, once Lady Mountbatten asked Gandhiji, 'Now that India has won its independence, why do you want to continue to travel in a third class train compartment? You can fly'. Bapu's reply was, 'If I were to use an aeroplane, how will I be able to meet the ordinary folk for whom I live and work?'

Yes, he was full of obstinate idiosyncrasies. But he was a great soul, a true 'Mahatma' who attached great importance to prayer. Every single day of his life commenced with prayer and ended with it too. He described prayer as the key to the morning and the bolt to lock up the evening.

His paramount concern during the freedom struggle was Hindu-Muslim unity. He dedicated his entire life trying to transform communal hatred into communal brotherhood. He criticised the behaviour of both the Hindus and the Muslims. At one time, he was portrayed as the enemy of the Muslims. But when he castigated the Hindus for their misdemeanours, he became the enemy of the Hindus. The fact remains that he was the enemy only of wrongdoing. He was incapable of hating anybody.

But the India of Gandhiji's dreams remains as remote as it ever was. He used to say, 'Swaraj doesn't mean some people rule over us. Real Swaraj means, people must be able to resist authority and throw out the wrong.'

Had Gandhiji been alive today, he would not have recognised this India. And even if he did, he would not have liked what he saw. He was a disheartened man within months of independence. There were complaints galore against the government, and his critics blamed him for their plight. He said, 'My voice is in the wilderness. My writ runs no more. The government does not listen to me. I am not the current coin that I fancied I once was.'

Had he been alive today, he would have started a revolution. He would have asked people not to vote for the corrupt politicians. We need a New India, an India devoid of corruption. Gandhiji wrote in the *Harijan*, dated 8 December 1946, that those who preferred security to freedom had no right to live.

Many valiant Gandhians have died unwept, unsung and unhonoured by the present generation. They never swerved from the Gandhian path and did not even opt for the pension offered to freedom fighters. The likes of such people are too few and far between in the current milieu.

I never claimed that I was a freedom fighter and never tried to get the freedom fighter's pension and other benefits. I joined

Bapu to serve the country, and not because I expected a reward in return. I was satisfied with the basic amenities I received for working with and for him; I mastered the art of good living with the minimum expense by emulating his example. As he loved to say, I eat to live and not live to eat.

It is with a sense of anguish and shame that I look at myself as a citizen of India today. I have an unconcealed contempt for the country and its people; a contempt that grows with each passing day.

I blame the politicians, the police, the judiciary and the bureaucracy for all of the ills of this country. I hold all four responsible for the dismal state of affairs of the nation.

Ideally, we should have a two- or three-party system—the Left, the Right, and a third Centrist party like the Swatantra Party.

I remember a private conversation between Rajaji and RR Divakar. When Divakar told Rajaji that they should propagate the ideals of Mahatma Gandhi among the youth of the country, Rajaji remained silent for a while and said, 'You will be wasting your time, energy and resources if you try to do anything of that sort. It will fall on deaf ears. It is enough if there are a dozen people in the whole of India who can lead the Gandhian way of life without bothering themselves with whether the world takes note of it or not.'

Rajaji said this decades ago, but it is truer today than it was then.

Mahatma had no enemies—not even the British, many of whom were his very dear friends and they helped him in his struggle for independence. He was opposed only to British rule. His letters to the Viceroy were addressed to a 'Dear Friend'.

The passing away of Mahatma Gandhi was the end of an epoch and the beginning of another. Long after his achievements in the political and social field have been forgotten, he will be remembered as an apostle of truth and love; a saint in a line of succession that runs through Buddha, Christ and Ramakrishna Paramhamsa.

But for now, Mahatma Gandhi has been reduced to a portrait on the wall, a forgotten figure. While Nehru's birthday is celebrated as Children's day, and Sarveppalli Radhakrishna's birthday as Teachers' day, we declare a holiday for Mahatma Gandhi's birthday. **Why can't we observe 2 October as cleanliness day**? That will be the best way to remember him and the best tribute we could give him.

Corruption

If corruption were an Olympic event today, India would win the gold medal. There's no doubt about it. But corruption did not start yesterday or today; its beginnings are in the immediate aftermath of independence. I attach most personal blame for this on the person of our first Prime Minister, Pandit Jawaharlal Nehru. Though he was personally a man of integrity, he took no action whatsoever against the corrupt people that surrounded him on all sides.

I am reminded of something that happened during the time of the 1948 Jeep Scandal [when the Indian High Commissioner to the UK, VK Krishna Menon, who went to become the Defence Minister of the country, was implicated in the signing of a Rs 80 lakh defence contract with a foreign firm].

In addition to Menon, there were corruption charges levelled against TT Krishnamachari [the first cabinet minister in independent India to have resigned due to allegations of his complicit involvement in the 1956 Mundhra scandal] and three others. But he never took a stance against any of them either.

A Member of Parliament questioned Nehru about his inaction in the matter, 'Sir, there is so much corruption everywhere, but why aren't you taking any action against anyone?'

Nehru's reply to the MP was telling. He replied, 'The Honourable Member should not be worried and need not make a fuss about a little corruption here and there.' To this, the MP gave a befitting repartee, 'Sir, a little corruption is like a little pregnancy. It keeps growing.'

How true! And look how it has grown!

Although all of our political parties constantly accuse each other of corruption, hardly anyone is punished. When A is in power, B is a criminal and when B is in power, A is a criminal.

If the corruption cases in our courts were decided in weeks rather than decades, very few people would dare to be corrupt. Today, legal action taken against the corrupt only helps the lawyers enrich themselves.

In my opinion, if our country is to progress and its citizens are to live in peace, the assets of the corrupt should be confiscated, and the corrupt and anti-social elements should be deported to the Andaman Islands for life, with no phone or travel facilities. Also, none of their family members should be permitted to enter politics for at least five generations!

Swachch Bharat

I am to cleanliness what Sachin Tendulkar is to cricket and Viswanathan Anand is to chess. Their records may not stand the test of time, but mine certainly will. In my letter to the present

Prime Minister, Narendra Modi, I wrote that I was very confident that nobody could ever beat my cleaning record. I have been cleaning from the age of eight; that means I have been doing this for the last eighty-five years!

They say cleanliness is next to Godliness. But I'll go one step further—I believe it is godliness that is next to Cleanliness. I have no faith in God; my faith rests in cleanliness. Neither do I believe in any religion and nor do I belong to one. I don't go to any temple. I worship work: every morning, I start my prayers at three by writing Sree Rama Jayam, Allahu Akbar and Jesus never fails.

I learnt many things from the British when I was a child and youngster. One of the most important things I did gather from them was my love or passion for cleanliness. Even Bapu used to say that he learnt the laws of cleanliness from the British. His words were, 'However much I may criticise the British, I must admit that I learnt the laws of sanitation from the Englishman.'

I have been spending every day of my life cleaning my own premises. Cleaning fills my stomach; sometimes, I even go without food for three days. If everything is clean, I feel like I've had a good meal.

Though Mahatma Gandhi spoke about this cleanliness and orderliness, nobody listened. That is why he had to go on speaking about it till the end of his life.

I feel a leader must have an iron hand to order things to be done, otherwise nothing is going to work in this country. That is why I feel, unless Narendra Modi is very strict about cleanliness, we will not become a Swachch Bharat.

What you have to do is to force the person who has to clean to do it. You should make every household responsible for its surroundings. The corporation is responsible for the main roads. It is the corporation's, panchayat's and municipality's duty to clean the roads. A Prime Minister cannot be directly involved in the cleanliness of the whole of India.

Like they do in foreign countries, cleaning the streets should be done at night; from 11 pm to 4 am.

The one place in India that I found spotlessly clean was Baba Ramdev's ashram. That is how the entire country should be.

Patel and Nehru

Comparisons are inevitable between Sardar Vallabhbhai Patel and Pandit Jawaharlal Nehru. This debate has its origins in the days before we were an independent nation. Incredibly, it continues to this day, even after almost seven decades of independence.

The very first time I met Patel was in 1945 when he came to the Sevagram Ashram. From then on, I was in touch with him regularly, and continued even after he became the Deputy Prime Minister of independent India. He was so great a man that I couldn't bring myself to discuss anything with him; not even politics. But when he used to visit Bapu at Birla House as the Deputy PM, I used to tell him of what I saw in the refugee camps, and he always listened intently to what I had to say.

The first impression I had of Patel was that he was a very strong man. Even then, he was known as the Iron Man. He was a man of action and got things done, once he decided upon them. In this respect, he was quite unlike Nehru.

Whenever a conflict between the Hindus and Muslims arose, Patel took the side of the Hindus but Nehru was always with the

Muslims. But you cannot call them communal. Patel used to say, 'I don't mean any disrespect to the Muslims, but if they are wrong, I will say so.' In fact, the differences of opinion between Patel and Nehru arose out of this difference in perspective. Even Gandhiji was aware of this difference. Though he never spoke of it openly, everyone knew it was on his mind.

Bapu chose not to take sides in this fight, as he knew both men were indispensable to the new nation. Patel had rendered yeoman service by consolidating the mish-mash of Princely States into the Union, while Nehru projected a secular image of India to the world.

It is widely believed that Gandhiji preferred Nehru as the Prime Minister and had even declared him as his political heir. But the truth is quite different. Mahatma Gandhi was too great a democrat to name anybody as the Prime Minister of an independent India. He wanted the people to decide upon their leader. He used to say, 'In a democracy, it is the people who matter, and I am nobody.' It was the Congress Working committee and its members who elected Nehru as the Prime Minister. This had nothing to do with Bapu.

Yes, he once said, 'Rajaji is my conscience keeper and Nehru my political heir.' People mistook this comment. When he said that, people thought he wanted Nehru to be the Prime Minister. No, that was not what he meant. Bapu did not expect to live long enough to see an independent India. Though he expected to live to be 125, he believed he would die before India won its independence. So I believe, what he meant was that he expected Nehru to carry on the struggle for independence in the event of his death. Perhaps Bapu chose Nehru as his political heir because

Nehru, unlike Patel, was well known around the world. Nehru was handsome and twenty years younger than Patel.

I knew Nehru from 1944 on. While I think Nehru had good ideas, he was a man of inaction. Having met him and heard him talk to Bapu, I expected him to do something more for the country. I thought he would stop corruption, but he did not take any action against the corrupt people in his government. If he had done that, he would have been the best Prime Minister the world had seen.

Nehru was also a man of short temper. After the Congress won only one out of the four seats it contested in by-elections in 1953, there arose a war of words between Syama Prasad Mukherjee and Nehru in Parliament.

'However much the Prime Minister may mistrust us or decry us, we also have a little hold in this country. In these elections, I saw with my own eyes how powerfully the sources of the government could be made to operate for the purpose of winning elections… money and wine played their parts in various spheres', said Shyama Prasad Mukherjee.

When Nehru shouted, 'Disgraceful', Mukherjee replied, 'Yes, it was nothing but disgraceful.'

Nehru said indignantly, 'It was disgraceful to have brought in the course of this debate these wild, irresponsible and fantastic charges. This itself shows the nature of the entire speech and the mentality behind it.'

When Syama Prasad Mukherjee replied, 'His temper shows more than anything else his incapacity to rule over this country', Nehru retorted, 'I ask the gentleman on the other side to prove that or withdraw the remarks about wine and women.'

Mukherjee retorted vehemently, 'I never said, women. I never used that word. Women may have been used, I do not know. I said, money and wine.'

But Nehru was still angry and said, 'I ask the member to prove his irresponsible statement.'

A sarcastic Syama Prasad Mukherjee said, 'It is no use losing your temper.'

When Nehru began, 'It is the Honourable member's right…', Syama Prasad Mukherjee replied, 'It is Jawaharlal Nehru's eternal right to lose his temper...'

It was not only Patel who complained about Nehru to Bapu; Nehru also complained about Patel. After one such incident, Patel offered his resignation. Bapu then asked him to come and meet him. That was on the 30th of January and it turned out to be their last meeting.

Bapu did not say anything about Patel being pro-Hindu. I heard him say this. 'I know there are differences between the two of you, but both of you are indispensable to the country. You have offered your resignation but I am not going to accept it. He has also offered his resignation but I will not accept that either. The two of you must work amicably. Don't blame any community and don't have any animosity towards Nehru. For good governance and for the sake of the country, you must remain united.'

It was after that meeting that Bapu was assassinated. From that day on, because Bapu was not there to stop their fights, Nehru and Patel perhaps decided to stay united. In a way, his death brought them together. Otherwise, they would have been fighting all the time.

Had Patel been the first Prime Minister, India would not have had any of the problems we have on her borders. Now China is after Arunachal Pradesh. This could have been avoided, had Sardar Patel been the Prime Minister. Nehru trusted China too much. It happened because of Krishna Menon. Nehru was a friend of Krishna Menon and he messed it up. Now China has occupied our territory. They are now siding with Pakistan too.

I will also blame Nehru for the blunder he committed in the case of Kashmir. Krishna Menon, Gopalaswamy Iyengar and Abdullah talked him into involving the United Nations. Nobody succeeded. Krishna Menon spoke for seven hours at a stretch. Here, people said, 'Ah, what a speech!' But there, everybody was sleeping. Somebody said, 'If it was such a strong case, he could have expressed it in seven seconds and not in seven hours.' Had Patel been the Prime Minister then, he would have gone to Kashmir, thrown out the occupiers and occupied the area. We have this country called India only because of Patel.

Maybe because Nehru belonged to Kashmir, he wanted to deal with it himself. He said, 'We will go to the United Nations.' That was the biggest mistake he made. When we went to the United Nations, we said that there was a dispute between India and Pakistan. But there was no dispute; they had trespassed into our territory! When you enter my house without my permission, you are called a thief. And when a thief enters your house, you first evict the thief from your house if you can, and only then do you call the police. So had Patel been given a free hand, he would have thrown out the thief and we would never have had any problems in Kashmir.

Experiments with Sex

One question I encounter all the time is about Bapu's experiments with sex. But my response to those who question Bapu's sexual proclivities is this: they should understand that Bapu's life was an open book, and he did nothing on the sly.

Every single moment in his life was open to everyone. If he had wanted to hide what he was doing from others, he could have locked himself up in his room as he carried out his experiments. But the doors to his room were always open, and nothing was hidden from anyone.

Yes, I feel he need not have done those sex experiments. With that, he spoilt his name unnecessarily. I can assure you that there were no bad intentions behind the sex experiments. One fine day, he started this experiment and justified it, even though nobody agreed with him.

It was sometime in February in 1947 when we were in Naokhali that this idea came to his mind. What he did was that he decided to sleep—be it during the day or at night—with women on either side of him. It was all in the open. Anybody could go into his room and see what he was up to. Nothing was concealed from anyone. That was how people came to know about it. If he had done it hiding inside his room, nobody would have had any knowledge of it.

Manu Gandhi was one of the women who lay down with him. Many people tried to persuade her not to do so, but she paid no heed to start with. But when she stopped doing so, Sushila Nayyar took her place.

When the others came to know of this, everybody was horrified. Among those who objected were Rajaji, his own son Devdas Gandhi, and some of the people who were with us in the ashram.

Bapu was unperturbed by all this. He said, 'My mind is clear. I am not doing anything wrong, it is all in the open. Those who want to leave may leave. I have nothing to hide.'

When Rajaji wrote him a letter objecting to these experiments, he wrote back thus on the 21st of February 1947:

> My Dear CR,
>
> This is with reference to the sleeping of Manu with me. I wanted to write to you earlier, but want of time put it off. Devdas is my strong opponent. I honour him for it but so far as I can see he has overreached himself this time. That my step may still be wrong is too true. Only his argument falls flat on me. If you feel like it, discuss it with him. If you don't feel like it, you need not. Nor are you bound in any way to give a thought to this unless you feel that you have something helpful to say against my step. I assume that you are opposed to the step. My simple argument is this: I have for years held it to be quite proper for a brahmachari that I claim to be, to share the same bed with his own daughter, if the occasion in his opinion demands it. Such an occasion is there in my case. This proposition might be held wrong initio. Then it will be difficult to dissuade me. How about the political situation?
>
> Love Bapu

Personally speaking, though I was very young, I wasn't too concerned about what he did, and I didn't feel the need to leave the ashram. Yes, it was objectionable and I still maintain that he needn't have done so. He wanted to show to people that he was above everybody else and could control his desires.

As far as I was concerned, it was just another experiment, like so many others he had done in his life. But Parasuram was so upset with what Bapu did that he left his service. But I continued.

I would not say, he set a bad example for others. He thought everybody was as great or as honest as he was. He would not do anything wrong as he had the willpower. But what Bapu didn't realise was that if a young man were to imitate him, it would lead to disaster.

His experiments continued for nearly a month and then he stopped, perhaps satisfied with his own willpower. What else could anyone do but bear with his idiosyncrasies?

I have with me another letter written by Bapu to Rajaji on the 6th of March 1947, when we were in Patna.

He wrote:

> My Dear CR,
> Your two previous letters [sic]. You are all good. You are all dear ones. But I fancy that you don't understand me, or it may be that I don't understand myself. The test you quote are before me [sic]. Only they don't lay down a universal code of conduct. But let time be the judge. Perhaps today it is not a burning

question, seeing that Manu has yielded to Bapa and no longer shares the bed with me. But that does not solve the question.

Love Bapu

The Prime Ministers of India

Pandit Jawaharlal Nehru

As the first Prime Minister of India, Nehru's greatest achievement was to make India a secular state. Though his administration was poor because of his strong personal likes and dislikes, he was a visionary. Only a visionary could think of doing things like building dams to improve Indian agriculture. But he went wrong in dealing with China and Pakistan. For instance, as everyone knows, he blundered in his handling of the Kashmir situation.

I would not describe him as a strong leader as he was not a man of action. Had he been a man of action, he would have thrown out all those corrupt people in his government immediately; he didn't do it. He only talked about corruption. He used to say, 'I will hang the black marketers by the nearest branch of the tree.' But black marketing went on. 'Aaram Haram Hain [to rest is sinful]', he said. But people rested all of the time. Nobody did any work. He was all talk, and enjoyed the applause.

Apart from these flaws, he was an ideal Prime Minister.

Lal Bahadur Shastri

I never had the occasion to meet Lal Bahadur Shastri as I don't remember him visiting Bapu.

He is a Prime Minister that history and this country has forgotten. But he was a great man nonetheless.

He ruled for just a year-and-a-half. Had he stayed alive longer, I am sure he would have achieved much more.

I am sure he would have done something against corruption as he was a clean man. When he died, he died penniless and didn't have any land to his name.

It was the same thing with Patel and Rajaji too. Patel passed away with just Rs 257 to his name when he died. Rajaji never made any money from politics, even if he was rich enough to have been the first man in South India to have owned a car. He was a great and successful lawyer, but gave it all up to join the freedom struggle.

Indira Gandhi

I had met her at Sevagram quite a few times and knew her very well. After independence, she used to come and see Bapu more. After visiting the refugee camps, she would come and report to Bapu what she had observed there.

I have talked to her a lot after independence. She had a very strong personality and was capable of convincing everybody of her point of view.

She did well also as a Prime Minister. People call her an autocrat but I don't agree; she was bold enough to dictate terms and take action against anyone.

People may also say she should not have imposed the Emergency [a 21-month period between 1975 and 1977 when Indira Gandhi, then Prime Minister, unilaterally imposed a state of emergency on the country and ruled by decree]. But I beg to differ. I see nothing wrong with the Emergency, even though people may say it was undemocratic. That was the only time in my memory that the people of India exhibited discipline, cleanliness and punctuality.

I remember what Subhash Chandra Bose said years before India won independence. He had said that there should be dictatorship in India for the first five years to set everything right. How right he was!

And we shouldn't forget her biggest achievement—winning the 1971 war with General Sam Manekshaw at the head of the military.

When we talk of the negatives of her time in office, her decision to let the army enter the sanctum sanctorum of the Golden temple [in 1983, as part of Operation Blue Star, to dislodge the Sikh militant Bhindranwale] ranks high on the list. Bhindranwale was once her friend. She nurtured him, thinking she could bring him around. But he turned the other way and became very strong. And thus it came to be that he was directly responsible for her death from beyond the grave.

While she wasn't a person of inaction like her father, she shared one trait with him; a tendency to turn a blind eye to corruption. She tried to justify this by saying that corruption was a worldwide phenomenon.

VP Singh, IK Gujral, Chandrashekar and Deve Gowda

I do not want to comment on VP Singh, Deve Gowda, Inder Gujral, and Chandrashekhar. There is nothing to say about them.

Rajiv Gandhi

Rajiv Gandhi came to power with a clean slate and he had a lot of goodwill. We were all so hopeful when he came to power that he'd stay clean. But I think a lot of us were disappointed at the end of his five years in office. As far as his widow, Sonia Gandhi is concerned, I don't think she would have succeeded as Prime Minister. She is just not Prime Minister material.

Atal Behari Vajpayee

Vajpayee was a good Prime Minister, a straightforward man. As a Prime Minister, he did well. His biggest achievement was building the highways that now connect India. Vajpayee was a man of action. He was not a man who could stay quiet, even for a minute.

I would say India started shining under him, but somehow, the slogan didn't work and these others [the Congress Party diarchy of Sonia Gandhi and Manmohan Singh] took over.

If he had got one more term, he would have done much more for the country. Unfortunately, they lost the election, and I believe that happened because of Advani. Lal Krishna Advani is more of a talker than he is a doer, and was consumed by his burning ambition to become India's Prime Minister.

If Modi had not won this time, and if Advani had become the Prime Minister instead, I don't think he would have done anything. Modi is a much better man than him.

Ten year diarchy of Manmohan Singh

Manmohan Singh was a good man, a man of integrity. I am sure he didn't make any money. But then again, he didn't appear to try and stop others under him from doing so. It has been alleged that all of his ministers made money right under his nose. It was like we had a new scam everyday.

I feel that he took orders only from Sonia Gandhi when he should have been asserting himself as a Prime Minister instead.

In my opinion, those ten years were the darkest and the most corrupt period in India's history. We didn't see allegations of corruption on such a massive scale before.

Narendra Modi

Narendra Modi, to me, is a 'no-nonsense Prime Minister'. That is because he doesn't tolerate the kind of nonsense we see all around us. But he will have to work hard to achieve a no-nonsense India.

He is also a man of action like Sardar Patel.

The Swachch Bharat scheme started by him is really laudable. As you are aware, I am fanatical about cleanliness. No Prime Minister until now has cared about this issue. They've never considered it important enough.

It is commendable that he spoke about Swachch Bharat and toilets in his first Independence Day speech. In our villages, people still relieve themselves in the open air. Building toilets for everybody should have been our top priority way back in 1947, but nobody seemed to care then. We're already sixty-eight years behind schedule on this, in my opinion.

He talks of bringing black [laundered] money back to India from their resting places abroad, but I have no idea whether he will succeed in this mission.

Modi has asked for five years to implement his ideas. Let's wait and see. That said, I believe he will succeed in turning his plans into reality only if he uses the power vested in him to make people work. I do not know how he will succeed when Gandhiji himself failed in spite of trying so hard, yet I am hopeful.

The biggest difference I see in him is that he comes from a poor family; he is an ordinary Indian while the others who came before him were not.

End Note

Kalyanam is an extraordinary man, just as extraordinary as the opportunity I had to speak with him for hours on end. He may sound unrealistic and impractical, but he is a man who has witnessed at close quarters the problems and challenges faced as India went from being a colony to an independent nation by way of a painful and bloody divorce.

Following the dawn of independence, he has lived under fifteen Prime Ministers—from Jawaharlal Nehru to Narendra Modi— some of whom he knew personally. Upon speaking to him, I realised he brought to the table a perspective on the Indian Republic that is fast disappearing from public discourse.

Very few get the opportunity like Kalyanam did, to walk amongst giants as they shaped the destinies of a subcontinent. As time passes, there are fewer and fewer like him left walking the face of the planet— men and women who bore close witness to some of Indian history's most tumultuous years.

Glossary

Cabinet Mission	The United Kingdom Cabinet Mission of 1946 to India was sent to the country to discuss and plan for the transfer of power from the British Government to Indian leadership.
Louis Francis Albert Victor Mountbatten, 1st Earl Mountbatten of Burma	Lord Mountbatten (1900 – 1979) Mountbatten, 1st Earl was a British statesman and naval Mountbatten of Burma officer, who served as the last Viceroy of British India and the first governor-general of the independent Dominion of India.
Pandit Jawaharlal Nehru	Nehru (1889 – 1964) was a nationalist politician who took active part in the freedom struggle,

and went on to become independent India's first elected Prime Minister.

Harijan — Translated into English as 'Child of Hari/Vishnu', Harijan was a term popularized by Mahatma Gandhi for referring to Dalits, traditionally considered to be untouchable. This term has now fallen out of favour, with many Dalit activists today considering the term condescending and insulting.

Rajendra Prasad — Rajendra Prasad (1884 – 1963) was a leader of the Indian independence movement, and subsequently served as the first President of the Republic of India from 1950 to 1962.

Pyarelal Nayyar — Pyarelal Nayyar (1899-1982) was one of Mahatma Gandhi's personal secretaries during his later years.

Sushila Nayyar — Sushila Nayyar (1914-2000) was Pyarelal Nayyar's sister and Mahatma Gandhi's personal physician

Khan Abdul Ghaffar Khan	Khan Abdul Ghaffar Khan (1890 -1988), also known as Badsha Khan and Frontier Gandhi, was a Pashtun leader and Indian nationalist. He was known for his nonviolence and pacifism.
Muhammad Ali Jinnah	Muhammad Ali Jinnah (1876-1948) was a lawyer, politician, and the founder of Pakistan.
Mirabehn	Mirabehn (1892–1982), born Madeleine Slade, daughter of the British Rear-Admiral Sir Edmond Slade, was a British woman who left her home in Britain to live and work with Mahatma Gandhi.
Mahadev Desai	Mahadev Desai (1892-1942) was Mahatma Gandhi's personal secretary for 25 years until his death in jail in 1942.
Mahar community	A community largely found in Maharashtra, traditionally classed as untouchable.

Edwina Cynthia Annette Mountbatten, Countess Mountbatten of Burma	Lady Edwina Mountbatten, Countess (1901–1960), wife of Lord Mountbatten of Burma Mountbatten, was the last Vicerine of India.
Chakravarthy Rajagopalachari	C Rajagopalachari, better known as Rajaji (1878-1972) was the last Governor General of India
MO Mathai	MO Mathai (1909 – 1981) was Jawarhlal Nehru's personal assistant from 1946 until 1959, when he was forced to resign in the face of allegations of spying and the misuse of power.
Sardar Vallabhbhai Jhaverbhai Patel	Sardar Patel (1875-1950) was independent India's first Deputy Prime Minister and the Home Minister.
Rajkumari Amrit Kaur	Rajkumari Amrit Kaur (1889-1964) was the Health Minister of independent India's first cabinet.
Kasturba Mohandas Gandhi	Kasturba Gandhi (1869-1944) was Mahatma Gandhi's wife

Maulana Abul Kalam Azad	Maulana Azad (1888-1958) was an Indian Muslim scholar, indepdence activist, and the first Education Minister in independent India's first cabinet.
Allopathy	Modern scientific medicine
Brahmachari	A celibate
Darshan	Viewing/seeing/meeting, used in the context of meeting a great man.
Khadi	Hand-spun cotton
Khakhra	A dry unleavened bread
Pranam	Bending and touching someone's feet in salutation
Satyagraha	Non-violent non-cooperation movement
Swaraj	Self-rule

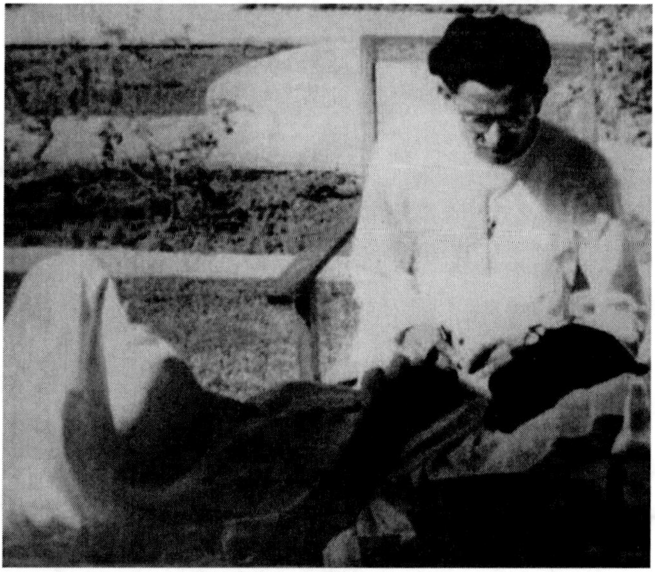

Bapu with Kalyanam (Upper)
Bapu, lying down and dictating to Kalyanam (Lower)

Bapu at work, Kalyanam is sitting next to him (U)
Bapu is listening to a visitor (L)

Bapu at the railway station with Abha

Bapu's body lies at rest. Kalyanam sitting at the right end

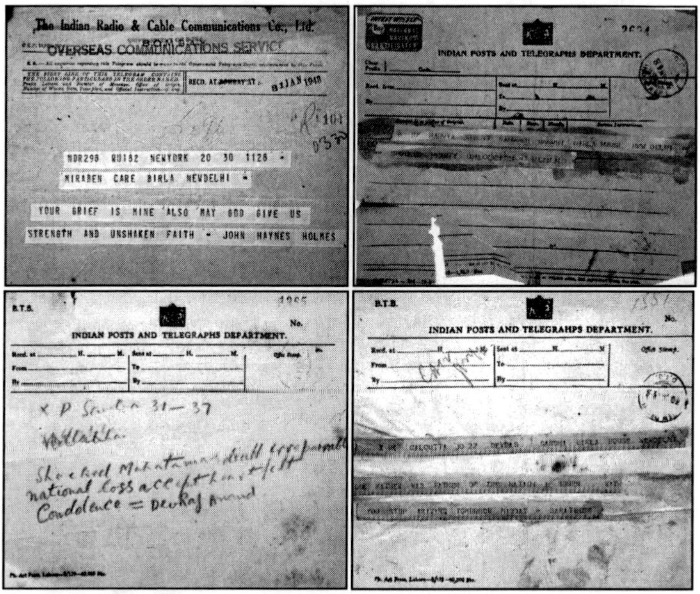
The Indian Radio & Cable Communications Co., Ltd.

OVERSEAS COMMUNICATIONS SERVICE

NDR298 RU152 NEWYORK 20 30 1128

MIRABEN CARE BIRLA NEWDELHI

YOUR GRIEF IS MINE ALSO MAY GOD GIVE US STRENGTH AND UNSHAKEN FAITH - JOHN HAYNES HOLMES

INDIAN POSTS AND TELEGRAPHS DEPARTMENT.

INDIAN POSTS AND TELEGRAPHS DEPARTMENT.

national loss accept heartfelt Condolence = Devraj Anand

INDIAN POSTS AND TELEGRAHPS DEPARTMENT.

The telegrams that reached Birla House after the Mahatma was assassinated, one of which was from his own son, Harilal

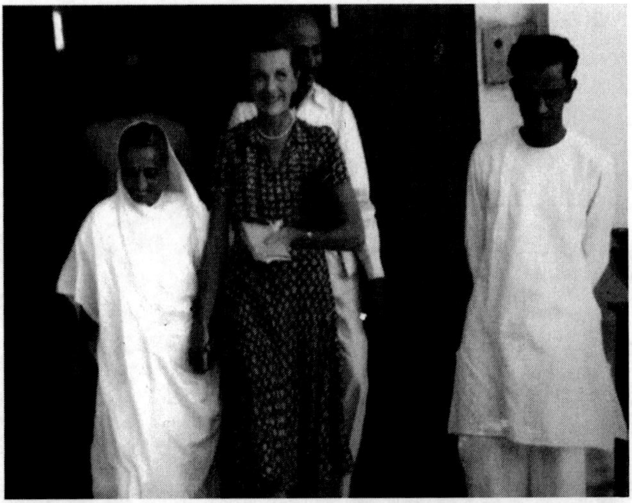

Kalyanam with Lady Mountbatten (U)
Rajaji at Kalyanam's wedding (L)

Khan Abdul Ghaffar Khan was a regular visitor at Sevagram and Banghi colony. There was a hut for him at Sevagram
Ghaffar Khan with Kalyanam's daughters in 1969 (inset)

a. Kalyanam with some of the letters written by Bapu
b. The front door of Kalyanam's house
c. Kalyanam at the Wardha station after many years, when he visited Sevagram.
d. e. f. Kalyanam at Sevagram

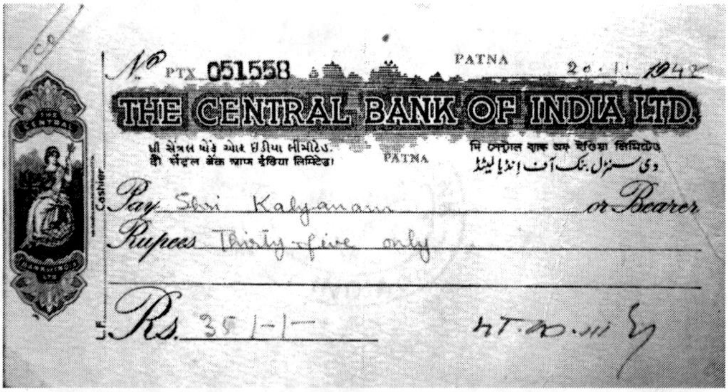

No. PTX 051558

PATNA

THE CENTRAL BANK OF INDIA LTD.

PATNA

Pay Sri Kalyanam or Bearer

Rupees Thirty-five only

Rs. 35/-/-

The cheque signed by Mahatma Gandhi in 1947 (U) Kalyanam with his daughters and grand children, with APJ Abdul Kalam (L)

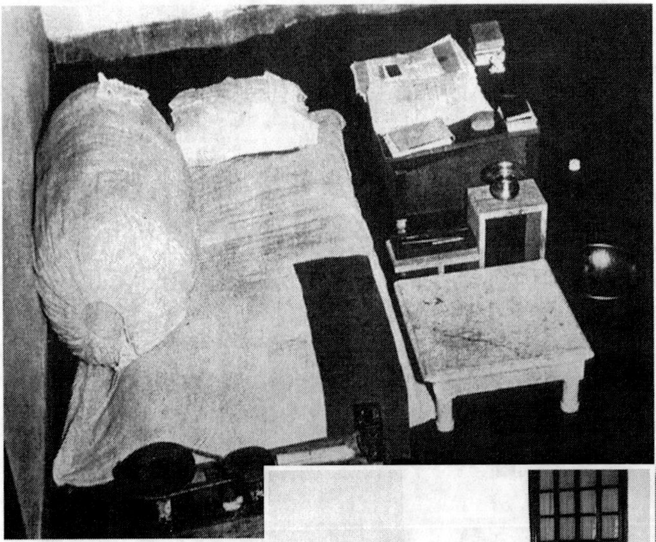

Bapu's room at
Birla House

Bapu's hut at
Sevagram